Rice and Revolution

*The Great Famine of Vietnam during
the Second World War, 1944-1945*

Pacific Atrocities Education

Rice and Revolution

The Great Famine of Vietnam during the Second World War, 1944-1945

Rijuta Vallishayee
Tessa Delgo

Rice and Revolution
*The Great Famine of Vietnam during
the Second World War, 1944-1945*

Written by
**Rijuta Vallishayee
and Tessa Delgo**

Editor
Stacey Anne Baterina Salinas

Published by Pacific Atrocities Education

All rights reserved. Printed in the United States of America. No part of this book may be reproduced in any manner whatsoever without written permission except in the case of brief quotations embodied in critical articles and reviews. For information, address Pacific Atrocities Education, 1693 Polk Street #1070, San Francisco, CA 94109.

Paperback ISBN: 978-1-947766-40-2
E-book ISBN: 978-1-947766-39-6

Table of Contents

Introduction	1
The French Colonial Period	9
French Conquest of the Mekong Delta	9
The History of the French Conquest of the Red River Delta and the Delta's Historical Context	11
Anti-Colonial Resistance	17
The Great Depression and Its Effects on Indochina	22
The Rise of the Communist Movement	24
The Nghe Tinh Soviet Movement	26
The Popular Front and the Beginning of the Second World War	29
1940: Imperial Japan's Entry into Indochina Comes to a Head	34
1941: The Rice Accords and the Formation of the Viet Minh	38
1942: The Intensification of Agricultural Exploitation	41
1943: The Portents of Famine	44
The Famine (1944-45)	49
Examining the Causes and Influences that Led to the Famine	57
Geography	57
About the Allocation of Blame	60
About the Impact of Natural Disasters and Agricultural Fallout	64

The French Role in the Famine	64
Imperial Japan's Role	70
The Consequences and Aftermath	74
Total Devastation: Statistics of the Estimated Deaths	75
Moves Towards Independence and the Rise of the Viet Minh	76
Conclusion: The Long-Term Effects and Legacy of the 1944-45 Vietnam Famine	84
Bibliography	**91**

Introduction

The word for "country" in Vietnamese is *đất nước*, literally "land and water." This is no descriptive coincidence. Land and water are the two components necessary for the cultivation of wet rice, Vietnam's staple crop. The two main regions of Vietnamese settlement surround rivers, where land and water come together to form the perfect conditions for rice cultivation. *Đất nước* may have originally referred to inland water systems like the Red River and the Mekong River, and the interplay between the land and salt water, specifically considering Vietnam's proximity to the strategically important South China Sea.

The relationship between *đất* and *nước* is a consistent theme in Vietnamese history, from their prehistory to Chinese domination, and Vietnamese independent dynasties. France pursued Vietnam's *đất nước* during the nineteenth century, leading to the establishment of the colony of French Indochina and over half a century of colonial exploitation. During the Second World War, Imperial Japan saw Vietnam as a source of rice to feed its army and people across Asia. The Great Famine of 1944-1945 is inseparable within this context of the exploitation of *đất* and *nước*. Though a rarely discussed aspect of the Second World War, this famine played an integral role in the story of the Vietnamese people's economic exploitation and their fight for sovereignty over their own *đất nước*.

The Great Famine of 1944-1945 took the lives of approximately one million people, about eight percent of Vietnam's population at the time.[1] Though the famine was directly ignited by a series of typhoons that destroyed an already weak harvest, there are two different narratives that run through the history of the famine. One focuses on the intrusion of colonial powers into Vietnam and their attempts to control Vietnam's land and water, while the other focuses on the resistance of the Vietnamese people.

The establishment of French Indochina in 1886 was the culmination of a decades-long French endeavor to obtain Vietnam's numerous natural resources. Through the tumultuous years of the late nineteenth and early twentieth century, the French colonial regime established powerful regional governments in the northern, central, and southern parts of modern Vietnam. To establish control, they extracted natural resources and exploited the labor of the Vietnamese people. The French also expanded the acreage of farmland and superficially managed the complex irrigation and dike

---

1. Gregg Huff, "Causes and consequences of the Great Vietnam Famine, 1944-5," *Economic History Review*, 00, 0 (2018), p. 1.

system that protected the farmers of Vietnam, especially northern Vietnam, from failed harvests.

After the defeat of France and the advent of the Vichy movement during the Second World War, Imperial Japan entered the region and coerced the Vichy government into a program of extreme extraction that pushed the Vietnamese people to the brink of starvation. After four years of extremely exploitative practices, it took just one year of drought and flooding to ignite a devastating famine. After the Japanese military carried out a coup against the Vichy government on March 9, 1945, they continued to carry out French policies until they were overthrown by the Viet Minh in August of that year.

While this narrative is certainly important for understanding why the famine was so devastating, it also erases the role of the Vietnamese people themselves. During the years leading up to the Second World War and the famine, a tide of resistance rose up against the French colonial machine. The famine would eventually play an important role in the initial liberation of Vietnam in 1945, as it boosted Vietnamese support for the nascent Viet Minh.

The Viet Minh was an organization built on the efforts of two generations of Vietnamese intellectual resistance. The first generation of intellectual resistance was diverse and varied ideologically, however, many leaders of the movement initially turned to Imperial Japan as an example of Asian independence. The second, eventually successful, generation of intellectual resistance was introduced to communism through the work of Nguyen Ai Quoc, more commonly known as Ho Chi Minh. In 1941, Ho Chi Minh and his allies adopted the popular front strategy and formed the Viet Minh. Utilizing traditional Vietnamese social structures, Ho was able to harness the power of the Vietnamese peasant class by turning communism into a promise for the delivery from exploitation. Using the surrender of the Japanese on August 14, 1945, the Viet Minh was able to initiate a coup and turn their well-organized revolutionary apparatus into the provisional government for the newly founded Democratic Republic of Vietnam (DRV).

The famine is often discussed as a mere aspect of the rise of the Viet Minh, a factor that contributed to their popular support and success. However, the suffering and resilience of the Vietnamese people during a time of extreme agrarian and civil unrest cannot be erased. Vietnamese voices expressing their experiences during the famine are a crucial part of the history surrounding the famine, which should be highlighted.

Both of these narratives tend to reduce the experience of the Vietnamese people, especially when they are written by non-Vietnamese authors, viewing the conflict within Vietnam during the 1940s from the outside. The English language literature on the famine, though somewhat scant, was created by a combination of non-Vietnamese and Vietnamese writers. The most comprehensive English language book which focuses primarily on the famine is *Rice Wars in Colonial Viet-*

nam: The Great Famine and the Viet Minh Rise to Power (2014), written by Geoffrey C. Gunn. *Rice Wars in Colonial Vietnam* discusses the famine and political developments in Vietnam in tandem, with a focus on the political and economic developments that led to the famine and the Viet Minh coup. Outside of *Rice Wars in Colonial Vietnam*, there are a number of books that discuss the famine in the context of the Viet Minh's rise to power, as well as a number of academic journal articles. The majority of these articles skew towards the economic, and many of them aim to elucidate the causes of the famine or assign blame to the various governments involved in Vietnam in the 1940s. Later in this work, we survey the literature and discuss the various perspectives surrounding blame for the famine in detail.

However, most of the literature about the famine remains in Vietnamese. *Nạn đói năm 1945 ở Việt Nam— Những chứng tích lịch sử* (*The 1945 Famine of Vietnam: Historical Records and Evidences*) is one of the definitive texts discussing the famine. The authors of this text, Van Tao and Furuta Motoo, center on the oral history of the famine, and the book was utilized by many English language authors to craft their own narratives.

There are a number of sources in French and Japanese as well, particularly due to the fact that many of the primary sources concerning the famine are located in French or Japanese archives. Unfortunately, we were unable to utilize many non-English language sources due to the language barrier. However, this publication utilizes numerous Vietnamese language primary sources, many of which were translated into English during their publication. Additionally, many of these Vietnamese language primary sources are easily accessible on the Internet, indicating that the famine was never forgotten in Vietnam.

Despite this, the famine remains relatively invisible on an international scale. The lack of English language sources is one of the reasons why this famine lacks visibility even though millions of people died as a result of it. The question remains as to why this is not often covered in English-language academia, or even in other English-language media. As mentioned earlier, when the famine is discussed in English language media, it is often described as a mere factor in the Viet Minh's rise to power. It is possible that the political events of the period, especially those involving global powers such as Vichy France and Imperial Japan, overshadowed the atrocity of the famine.

However, the famine's scope demands that it should be addressed in its own right. The sheer scale of death of this famine exists within a greater context, one involving the deadly intersection of French and Japanese colonialism. This context remains relevant to the lives of the Vietnamese people today. As of 2021, the famine took place seventy-eight years ago. It is likely that famine survivors are still alive, and even if the majority of famine survivors have passed on, their children still live with the ramifications of their parents' health. A recent study showed that the famine "reduced literacy by around three percent, BMI by 5.6%-8.4%, arm-length by 4.5%-6.7% (1.1-1.7 cm), height by 2.2%-3.2% (3.4-5 cm), and weight by 10%-14% (4.7-6.9 kg)."[2] Therefore, these atrocities remain relevant to the modern day.

As the Great Famine of 1944-1945 remains remote to English speaking audiences, we aim to elucidate the context, events, and effects of this famine. Its causes and effects are relevant not only to the famine but also to understanding modern Vietnamese history. We place the famine in the context of Vietnamese geography, French colonialism and control of agricultural practices, the Second World War, and Vietnamese resistance against French and Imperial Japanese incursions. Understanding the famine is not just a matter of analyzing harvest totals and death counts. Therefore, we have chosen an approach that emphasizes two aspects of the famine: its historical context and its tragic scope. The latter aspect is often discussed through numbers, however, we have chosen to emphasize the narratives of Vietnamese famine survivors to both counteract the lack of Vietnamese secondary sources and emphasize to readers the loss of humanity that occurred during this time. As for the former aspect, the context for the famine could begin anywhere from the beginning of wet rice cultivation in the Red River Delta to the surrender of France to Germany in 1940. However, we chose to

---

2. Cahit Guven, Trung Hoang, Muhammad H. Rahman, Mehmet A. Ulubaşoğlu, "Long-term effects of malnutrition on early-life famine survivors and their offspring: New evidence from the Great Vietnam Famine 1944-45," *Health Economics* 30, Issue 7, p. 1600.

begin this narrative of the famine at the onset of the 1930s, which saw the advent of a pattern of French control over Vietnamese agriculture and subsequent Vietnamese agrarian unrest that would eventually escalate into extreme exploitation and the rise of the Viet Minh. In order to better understand the events of the 1930s, we begin with an overview of French colonialism and Vietnamese resistance before 1930, which reveals that while the Great Famine of 1944-1945 was a tragedy, it was certainly not an entirely unexpected one.

The French Colonial Period

French Conquest of the Mekong Delta

The two primary deltas of Vietnam.³

---

3. Rijuta Vallishayee, *The Two Primary Deltas of Vietnam*, map graphic, 2021.

The Great Famine of 1944-1945 cannot be separated from the context of French and Japanese colonialism. A thorough understanding of the French colonial project in Vietnam is necessary to understand the famine. By the year 1944, the institution of French Indochina had already existed for over half a century. It was through the south that the French first gained power in Vietnam, through the court of the Nguyen emperors. The French had been traveling to Vietnam since the seventeenth century, for the purposes of religious and colonial expansion. Military involvement began when a small number of French troops unofficially supported the first Nguyen emperor, Gia Long, during his bid for the throne.[4] French advisors remained present in the Nguyen court as it ruled Vietnam, and during the reign of Napoleon III, French ships began to shell central and southern cities such as Da Nang. In 1859, the French successfully took the southern city of Saigon, overturned the Nguyen court's export ban, and exported fifty-seven thousand tons of rice from the southern region known to them as Cochinchina.

The French prioritized the growth of agriculture in the Mekong Delta, and commenced land reclamation throughout the region. In addition to constructing irri-

---

4. The Nguyen Dynasty (1802-1945) was the final dynasty of Vietnamese monarchs. Gia Long was the first emperor of the dynasty, having defeated the previous Tay Son Dynasty and declared himself emperor in 1802.
Ben Kiernan, *Viet Nam: A History from Earliest Times to the Present* (New York: Oxford University Press, 2017), p. 263.

gation systems and canals, the French colonial government sold vast tracts of land to French *colons* (colonists) and Vietnamese dignitaries, altering the spectrum of land ownership throughout the region. Society grew more polarized, to the point where 72% of the total population owned no land, and only 2% of the total population owned approximately half of the land in 1930.[5] On large land holdings, rice was grown using a sharecropping system, while the few remaining small landowners farmed their own lands. The standard of living of tenants remained low, even as French Cochinchina exported as much as one million tons of rice every year.[6]

The History of the French Conquest of the Red River Delta and the Delta's Historical Context

The French turned their attention to the northern part of Vietnam, known to them as Tonkin, in the 1870s. French troops initially conquered Hanoi in 1873, and returned to fully conquer the city in 1882.[7] While Cochinchina was considered a colony under the French, Tonkin was initially labelled as a "protectorate," meaning that the region was still nominally ruled

---

5. J. F. Le Coq., M. Dufumier and G. Trébuil, "History of rice production in the Mekong Delta," *The Third Euroseas Conference* (London, 2001), p. 5.
6. Le Coq, Dufumier, and Trebuil, "History of rice production in the Mekong Delta," p. 3.
7. Kiernan, *Viet Nam*, p. 319.

by the Nguyen court at Hue until 1887. However, the region was effectively ruled by a French resident, who could demand audiences with the emperor.

Agriculture was not the primary priority of the French in Tonkin, who aimed to gain access to southern China and Tonkin's coal and mineral supplies during their first invasion.[8] This did not stop the French from attempting to develop a plantation economy in Tonkin, much like the one that they had developed in Cochinchina. However, by the time the French arrived in Tonkin, land in the arable Red River Delta was already greatly parceled.

The Red River Delta flows from the mountains of Yunnan, China, into the Gulf of Tonkin in northern Vietnam. The drastic elevation change between the river's source and its delta makes for a fast flowing, rapidly changing river. These changes only grew more dramatic beginning in the late seventeenth century, when mining began in areas near the river's source.[9] The stripping of sediment from settled mining regions turned the river red with sediment, leading to the river's modern name.

The Red River's high sediment content was deposited in its delta, leading to a constantly changing landscape. The delta's landscape has been regularly growing for four thousand years, opening more land for human

---

8. John F. Laffey, "Land, Labor and Law in Colonial Tonkin Before 1914," *Historical Reflections / Réflexions Historiques*, vol. 2, no. 2 (1976), p. 223. www.jstor.org/stable/41298668.
9. Tana Li, "A Historical Sketch of the Landscape of the Red River Delta," *Trans-regional and -national studies of Southeast Asia 4*, no. 2 (2016).

settlement in the western delta. The modern waterways of the delta were only established in the past three hundred years, emphasizing the dynamic nature of the landscape.[10] Due to the uneven deposition of sediments and the already present soil varieties of the region, the delta consists of distinct regions. In general, the central and lower delta, where the Red River deposited most of its sediments, is richer in nutrients.

Due to its more northern latitude, northern Vietnam experiences more distinct seasons than its southern counterpart. Broadly speaking, the wet season lasts from April to October, while the dry season lasts from November to March.[11] However, there is great regional variation within this pattern, and many regions, such as Hanoi, can distinguish four seasons. The delta also generally receives a preliminary rainy period during midwinter due to its northern latitude. The long rainy season, combined with the risk of typhoons during the same period and the fast flow of the Red River, contributes to a high risk of flooding in the Red River Delta.[12] According to the historical record, flood years are often followed by drought years.[13] The flood and drought cycle endanger crops grown in the delta, placing the population of the region at risk of famine.

---

10. Ibid.
11. Hurley, M. M., Minh, L. D., Sterling, E. J. (2008). *Vietnam: A Natural History.* Ukraine: Yale University Press.
12. Ibid.
13. Geoffrey C. Gunn, *Rice Wars in Colonial Vietnam: The Great Famine and the Viet Minh Road to Power* (Lanham, Maryland: Rowman & Littlefield, 2014), p. 33.

Humans have lived in the delta region since 14,000 BCE.[14] The archeological record is incomplete due to significant changes occurring in the northern region, including the submersion of a vast region of land, now under the Gulf of Tonkin. At about 2,000 BCE, the South China Sea receded to reveal the Red River's floodplain. Agriculture began in the hills surrounding the delta, where farmers used the slash-and-burn method to clear land. It was during Vietnam's Bronze Age, around 1,000 BCE, that wet rice agriculture began.[15] Due to the constant risk of flood, dikes and irrigation systems were utilized to control the flow of water. The irrigation systems in place during the French colonial period and afterwards "literally represented the accumulated labor of millions over history."[16]

The Red River Delta is also considered to be the location of the first Vietnamese kingdoms, with its capital in what is now Hanoi.[17] When the Chinese arrived during the Qin and Han dynasties, they conquered the northern and central regions and ruled from near modern Hanoi, leaving the central and southern parts of modern Vietnam to their Cham and Khmer rulers. When the independent Vietnamese kingdom of Dai Viet emerged after the collapse of the Song Dynasty in the tenth century, it controlled only the north and parts of the central region of modern Vietnamese and ruled from the capital of Hanoi, on the delta. Power over Vietnam was con-

---

14. Kiernan, *Viet Nam*, p. 26.
15. Ibid, p. 30.
16. Gunn, *Rice Wars*, p. 28.
17. Kiernan, *Viet Nam*, p. 35.

centrated in the hands of those who ruled the Red River Delta. Likewise, the delta has always held a large concentration of the Vietnamese population relative to its size. By the 1930s, one third of the Indochinese population lived in the delta, which only represented two percent of Indochina's land.[18] This meant that even before French conquest, land in the delta was highly parceled among small, midsized, and large landholders.

Although land on and near the delta was given to French *colons*, the sharecropping system utilized in Cochinchina did not work in Tonkin. This was because Vietnamese farmers in Tonkin lacked the motivation to become sharecroppers, and those who found their land under French control remained noncompliant in resistance.[19] Therefore, land in Tonkin remained highly parceled under the French, and the majority of its rural inhabitants were subsistence farmers who relied on smaller plots of land for food.

In addition to attempting to change the land parcelization of Tonkin, French authorities found the Nguyen administration's hydraulic management lacking.[20] As mentioned before, the system of dikes and canals in Tonkin represented centuries' worth of attempts to control the Red River's frequent floods. The condition of the dikes was especially crucial to preventing floods that would destroy harvests and devastate millions of Vietnamese

---

18. Gunn, *Rice Wars*, p. 28.
19. John F. Laffey, "Land, Labor and Law in Colonial Tonkin Before 1914," *ibid.*
20. Kiernan, *Viet Nam*, p. 209.

farmers. The French began to dike the Red River Delta in 1923.[21] While both Vietnamese and French constructed dikes were constantly widened and raised, the materials that were used left dikes vulnerable to erosion. They could break or be breached if floodwaters rose high enough or flowed fast enough. A similar situation occurred in the case of irrigation canals, crucial for alleviating famine caused by droughts. Periodical famines caused by the flood and drought cycle led to French consideration of an unprecedented delta-wide management program.

As in Tonkin, central Vietnam, known to the French as Annam, was designated as a protectorate. It was the last of the three regions of Vietnam to be incorporated fully into the French empire, remaining a rump state until resistance from royalist forces encouraged French forces to fully conquer the region. Though Annam and Tonkin were considered parts of French Indochina, they were nominally ruled by the Nguyen court from Hue, although real power lay in the hands of the French resident. This meant that the civil service in the protectorates remained in the hands of the Confucian scholar-officials. Vietnamese law remained in place, and the typical structures of Vietnamese rural life, such as the village, remained intact. The preservation of traditional social structures would prove crucial in the next decades, as Vietnamese leaders relied on community organization to resist the colonial regime.

---

21. Gunn, *Rice Wars*, p. 36.

A rough outline of the divisions between Tonkin, Annam, and Cochinchina.[22]

Anti-Colonial Resistance

Due to the maintenance of past social structures, much of the resistance against French colonialism took place in Annam and Tonkin. Military resistance began with the Can Vuong (Save the King) movement in Annam, however, this was defeated by Cochinchinese forces in 1882.[23] The last form of major military resistance against the French until after the Second World War took place in the hills of Tonkin, where Hoang Hoa Tham held out until 1913. From then on, the majority of anti-colonial resistance would be carried out on a different playing

---

22. Rijuta Vallishayee, *A Rough Outline of the Divisions Between Tonkin, Annam, and Cochinchina*, map graphic, 2021.
23. Kiernan, *Viet Nam*, p. 326.

field, led first by Confucian-educated intellectuals who passed their torch to educated, professional revolutionaries. The Annam provinces of Nghe An and Ha Tinh, collectively known as Nghe Tinh, were known for the revolutionary movements and leaders they produced.

French Indochina in the context of Southeast Asia, 1886[24]

24. In addition to the three regions of Vietnam, French Indochina also included much of modern day Cambodia and Laos, as well as parts of modern day China. "Map of Indochina Showing Proposed Burma-Siam-China Railway," *Scottish Geographical Magazine* (1886), ed. Hugh A. Webster and Arthur S. White.

Nghe An was the birthplace of one of the leaders of the first generation of intellectual resistance, Phan Boi Chau. Phan Boi Chau was studying for the Confucian civil service examinations when the Can Vuong movement collapsed, and he turned to the organization of a society that would further the cause of anti-colonial resistance. In 1904, he obtained the allegiance of the Nguyen Prince Cuong De, who he used as a rallying point for his organization, The Reformation Society (Duy Tan Huy).

Cuong De had received some support from Imperial Japan, and many first generation intellectual anti-colonialists also looked to Japan as a base for future activities and a model for reform.[25] This movement towards Japan was known as the Dong Du Movement. This first generation varied individually in terms of ideology, ranging from monarchist to republican. Despite these differences, the movement was distinctly nationalist, focusing only on anti-colonial resistance instead of a nationalist and proletariat revolution. Various groups based on different ideologies appeared and disappeared, but none were as influential as Phan Boi Chau's organization, nor as successful as the second generation of revolutionaries.

Although Phan Boi Chau lived much of his revolutionary career in exile or house arrest, he still influenced the second, ultimately successful generation of revolutionaries, led by the enigmatic Ho Chi Minh. Phan was a friend of Ho's father and influenced Ho's patriotism

---

25. Gunn, *Rice Wars,* p. 56.

when he was a child named Nguyen Tat Thanh.[26] Nguyen was educated in the Confucian tradition, though he was expelled from school as a teen due to his participation as a translator for peasant uprisings in Hue. Eventually, he left Vietnam in 1911 and travelled the world as a messboy on various French liners.[27] He settled in France after the end of the First World War, where he quickly became affiliated with the nationalist organizations founded by the first generation of revolutionaries in exile.

There, he founded a nationalist group called the Association of Annamite Patriots with the help of first generation anti-colonialists Phan Chu Trinh and Phan Van Truong. This organization, like many other nationalist groups in Paris at the time, sought to take advantage of the Versailles Peace Conference happening at the time (Duiker chapter 2) Ho, with the help of his colleagues, wrote an eight-point declaration demanding equality under the law for both the Vietnamese and French people, freedom of speech, religion and assembly, amnesty for Vietnamese political prisoners, and Vietnamese representation in the French government.[28] This declaration was called "Revendications du Peuple Annamite," and it was signed by Nguyen Ai Quoc, the most famous of Ho's numerous names. Ho was responsible for publicizing the document, and he personally delivered it to both the

---

26. William J. Duiker, *Ho Chi Minh: A Life* (United Kingdom: Hachette Books, 2000), Chapter 1.
27. Ibid.
28. Nguyen Ai Quoc, "Revendications du Peuple Annamite" (1919).

President of France and the Palace of Versailles, as well as published it in a socialist paper.

Nguyen Ai Quoc (Ho Chi Minh) at the French Communist Congress at Marseilles, 1921.[29]

---

29. Louis Meurisse, *Nguyen Aïn Nuä'C (Ho-Chi-Minh), délégué indochinois, Congrès communiste de Marseille*, 1921, Bibliothèque Nationale de France Gallica, https://commons.wikimedia.org/wiki/File:Nguyen_A%C3%AFn_Nu%C3%A4%27C_(Ho-Chi-Minh),_d%C3%A9l%C3%A9gu%C3%A9_indochinois,_Congr%C3%A8s_communiste_de_Marseille,_1921,_Meurisse,_BNF_Gallica.jpg.

Although he received notes from world leaders that his declaration had been received, nothing came of it. This was merely part of the trend of rejection of the Fourteen Points to reach compromises between the European powers, however, it did effectively mark one of the first official requests for basic liberties to be extended to the Vietnamese people, and the first missed chance at the peaceful attainment of such rights. France left the conference with its power in Indochina intact, setting the stage for the events of the next two decades.

The 1930s set the stage for the chaos and hardship faced by the Vietnamese people during the 1940s. By this time, French colonization had officially controlled all of Vietnam for over four decades. The 1930s saw the advent of the movements that would dominate the events of 1944 and 1945, from the official start of the communist movement in Indochina to large agrarian crises that would set a precedent for famine management in Tonkin. The year 1930 itself was pivotal in the development of the movements and institutions that would prove prominent in later decades.

The Great Depression and Its Effects on Indochina

The most notable global event of the year 1930 was the Great Depression. Areas that were more connected to the global economy through trade were more affected, meaning that French Indochina and its rice trade was influenced by the global depression. Prices began to fall around 1930 and recovered by 1934.[30] The fall in rice prices made it easier for rice buyers to purchase rice, but those who sold their surplus rice faced problems. Rice sellers had to make up for lost income and taxes by selling more rice than they usually would, and landlords and debtors kept up the pressure.[31]

Economically, the subsistence-based farmers of the north were less affected because they did not rely on exports. Tonkin did not lose much cultivated land in comparison to Cochinchina, though concessions were given up by both the French and Vietnamese landowners.[32] However, the overpopulation and high parcelization of land led to high unemployment rates. In addition to economic pressures, there were both floods and droughts during during 1930, affecting the rice harvest (Gunn 87).[33] The meager harvest, combined with the lower prices of rice, led to a food shortage in the region that caused famine in some areas of Annam and Tonkin. The events of the early 1930s must be considered within the context of food shortages and economic hardship caused by the depression that would continue to affect the Mekong Delta region as the Pacific theatre of the Second World War grew more intense.

---

30. Irene Nørlund. "Rice and the Colonial Lobby: The Economic Crisis in French Indo-China in the 1920s and 1930s." *Weathering the Storm: The Economies of Southeast Asia in the 1930s Depression*, ed. Peter Boomgaard and Ian Brown (Singapore: Institute of Southeast Asian Studies, 2000), p. 198.
31. Gunn, *Rice Wars*, pp. 86-87.
32. Nørlund, "Rice and the Colonial Lobby," p. 203.
33. Gunn, *Rice Wars*, p. 87.

The Rise of the Communist Movement

Perhaps one of the most important events of 1930 was the formation of the Indochinese Communist Party (ICP) in the February of that year. The success of the ICP in 1945 was predicated on the specific condition of the anti-colonial movement in Vietnam during the 1930s and 1940s. In addition to the communists' message of liberation from the economic hardships of French colonialism, the lack of a coherent rival organization made it easier for the ICP to expand its influence.[34] The Yen Bai Mutiny in February 1930 coincided with the foundation of the ICP, just as it removed the ICP's greatest rival organization.

The Vietnamese Nationalist Party (VNQDD) embodied the first generation of revolutionaries' philosophies, and was founded in 1927. Based on the model of the Kuomintang (KMT) in China, it was ideologically confused but traditionalist in nature.[35] Despite its ideological confusion, the VNQDD remained a rival to the infant communist movement in Vietnam. However, their penchant for violence in the quest for independence led to their downfall. First, the assassination of the director of the General Office of Indochinese Manpower in 1929 led to a French-led purge of the VNQDD's regional sections.[36] After the destruction of numerous cadres due

---

34. Huỳnh Kim Khánh, *Vietnamese Communism, 1925-1945* (Ithaca: Cornell University Press, 1982), p. 103.
35. Ibid, p. 93.
36. Ibid, p. 95.

to political violence, the party planned one last act of rebellion in the garrison of Yen Bai. However, the French were already informed of the mutiny, and it was easily squashed within a day (Kiernan 364).[37]

This led to the destruction of the VNQDD, as the leaders of the organization were quickly arrested after the failed mutiny. For the infant communist movement, the fall of the VNQDD proved that revolution without a specific ideology was doomed to fail. Additionally, it meant that the communist movement had no other ideological or major organizational rival, which led to communist domination of the anti-colonial movement.

Meanwhile, the communist movement itself was gaining traction as it developed from a number of small movements into a singular party. Up until 1930, Vietnam did not have one communist party. In general, there were two primary groups of communists: the League of Vietnamese Revolutionary Youth (known as the Thanh Nien and founded by Nguyen Ai Quoc) and the Indochinese Communist League (founded by followers of Phan Boi Chan and called the Thanh Viet).[38] The former split in two 1929, and Nguyen Ai Quoc convened a conference in Hong Kong in the name of the Comintern (Communist International) to unify the parties.

In February 1930, the factions agreed to unite and named themselves the Vietnamese Communist Party. However, the party was soon reprimanded by Comintern and ordered to reform, so in October 1930, the party

---
37. Kiernan, *Viet Nam*, p. 364.
38. Ibid.

changed its name to the Indochinese Communist Party (ICP) and established their goals and programs, which were followed for the next several years.[39] Much of the organizational apparatus established at this First Plenum in October has remained unchanged up to the modern day. Unfortunately, coming out into the open meant that the party's leadership was exposed, and many leaders were placed in jail in 1931.[40] Due to the Comintern's greater involvement in the ICP in the following years, Nguyen Ai Quoc's influence in the party waned and the party itself experienced several years of internal struggle over the question of nationalism.[41] Nguyen himself was jailed in 1931 and was rumored to have died in prison.

The Nghe Tinh Soviet Movement

The rise of communist ideology and organizational apparatus in Vietnam was especially prominent in the traditionally belligerent provinces of Nghe An and Ha Tinh, collectively known as Nghe Tinh. After the Yen Bai rebellion and the founding of the ICP, revolutionary activity around the entire country increased under the eye of an increasing number of French troops.[42] This involved the dissemination of communist propaganda, strikes, and even the assassination of minor government

---

39. Khánh, *Vietnamese Communism*, p. 129.
40. Ibid, p. 59.
41. Ibid, p. 179.
42. Ibid, p. 153.

figures. However, the French authorities were more concerned with strikes and demonstrations in the more economically important south, so revolutionary activity in Tonkin and Annam, especially in Nghe Tinh, continued.

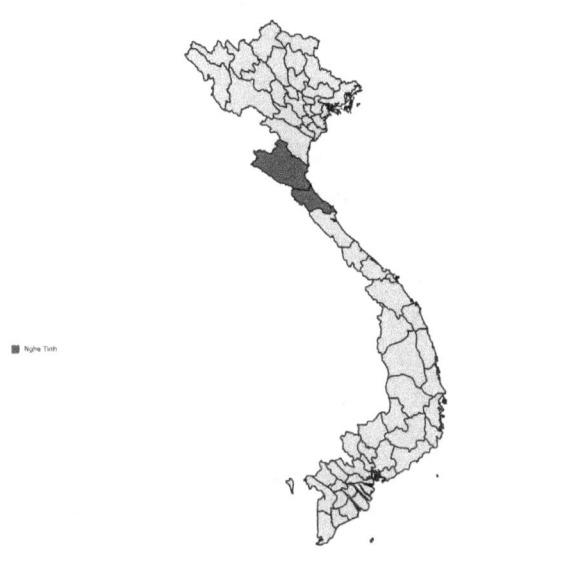

The provinces of Nghe An and Ha Tinh, collectively known as Nghe Tinh, are marked.[43]

This came to a head at the beginning of September 1930 when the French bombed a mass demonstration in Vinh, leading to one hundred and forty-one deaths and hundreds more being injured.[44] In the ensuing

---

43. Rijuta Vallishayee, *Nghe Tinh*, map graphic, 2021.
44. Martin Bernal, "The Nghe-Tinh Soviet Movement 1930-1931," *Past & present,* no. 92 (1981), p. 152.

chaos, many village leaders gave up their positions under pressure from peasant groups that were organized under the ICP and known as "soviets." Protests continued as French troops poured into Nghe Tinh to "pacify" the region. This involved razing soviet villages, as well as killing and deporting "rebels," meaning anyone who was caught by the French troops.[45]

The sheer brutality of the French troops led to the destruction of numerous villages and the deaths of thousands, leading to a backlash from French citizens. Although the government fired many important officials, many of their replacements were more brutal than their predecessors.[46] By the end of 1931, most communist cadres had been killed or disbanded in fear, and with the ICP's own leadership in shambles, communism in Vietnam had been dealt an almost fatal blow.

The Nghe Tinh Soviet Movement's significance lies in its economic and meteorological context and its foreshadowing of the political and economic situation in 1945. Unrest in Nghe Tinh was not simply predicated on the conception of the ICP. Instead, peasants latched onto communist ideology during a period of extreme hardship. Rice prices were at their lowest during 1931, and both the fall harvest of 1929 and the spring harvest of 1930 had failed. The combination of low amounts of paddy and low price led to famine in certain parts of Annam. Much of the unrest during 1930 and 1931 arose from "rice borrowing" expeditions, where rice

---

45. Khánh, *Vietnamese Communism*, p. 157.
46. Bernal, "The Nghe-Tinh Soviet Movement," p. 154.

was often violently redistributed from stocks to the poor.[47] Therefore, famine played an important role in the Nghe Tinh Soviet Movement, as a condition that enhanced the struggle against colonialism carried out by the Vietnamese people.

The role of famine in the Nghe Tinh Soviet Movement foreshadowed the role of famine in the August Revolution. However, the main difference between the August Revolution and the Nghe Tinh Soviet Movement lay in the scale of the movement and the organizational capability of the ICP. Without the degree of planning that went into the August Revolution, as well as the time that the ICP had to grow its organization's branches across Vietnam, the Nghe Tinh Soviet Movement was doomed. While bursts of uprising continued across Tonkin and Annam, such as the Annam Anti-tax Movement of 1932-1934, further rebellion was brutally crushed by the French. Mass arrests destroyed the ICP's fledgling organization, leading to a low point in the anti-colonial movement.

The Popular Front and the Beginning of the Second World War

1936 brought major changes to French Indochina, due to the election of the Popular Front government in France. This new government provided new opportu-

---

47. Ibid, p. 166.

nities for the anti-colonial movement in Vietnam, as well as an opportunity for the French government to prove its ability to handle agrarian crises. The Popular Front and the ICP were linked through their connection with Communist International (Comintern). In 1935, Comintern reversed its policy towards alliances with moderate and socialist policies, advocating for unity against the rising tide of fascism.[48] This enabled the French Communist Party to join with the French Socialist Party and other leftist parties to form a left-leaning government.

Within Vietnam, the temporary liberalization of the legislature saw the creation of another alliance, once between Stalinists and Trotskyists.[49] The primary difference between these two groups lay in their aims. While the Trotskyists were focused on ending imperialist capitalism, the Stalinists were focused on ending feudalism. Nevertheless, these two groups allied in Cochinchina under their newspaper, *La Lutte*, and achieved temporary success in regional elections, such as the Saigon Municipal Council elections of 1933, 1935, and 1937.[50]

Meanwhile, political prisoners, released by the Popular Front, led the beginnings of the revival of the ICP in Tonkin. The actions of these two groups led to mass support for Marxist candidates among the people of all three regions of Vietnam. However, the revival of

---

48. Kiernan, *Viet Nam*, p. 365.
49. Gunn, *Rice Wars*, p. 108.
50. Khánh, *Vietnamese Communism*, p. 199.

The front page of *La Lutte*, February 23, 1935.[51]

---

51. *La Lutte, February 23 1935*, 1935.

the ICP led to the dissolution of the *La Lutte* group in 1937.[52] Nevertheless, the non-ICP affiliated *La Lutte* group had eased the way for the ICP to form organizational networks in Cochinchina, due to the positive public opinion they had built up during their years in government. Factional disputes and leadership from Comintern made it difficult for the ICP to prepare fully for the revolution they claimed to be working towards.

Meanwhile, the whole of Vietnam experienced an agrarian crisis during 1936 and 1937. Rice prices had recovered to their pre-depression numbers by 1934, leading French officials to believe that the economy had fully recovered from the chaos of the first few years of the decade.[53] However, the monsoon rains came late in 1936, leading to a deficient spring 1937 harvest in Tonkin and Annam.[54] The same year, floods struck both the northern and southern parts of Vietnam, destroying rice fields. The Popular Front government took major steps to try to alleviate the hardship, by shipping rice from less affected areas to suffering regions, starting public works to provide jobs, and providing financial aid and rations, as well as loans and seeds for the recovery of cultivation.

The quick action taken by the government represented the culmination of the French capability for disaster management in Indochina. Although the 1936-1937 crisis proved that the colonial government was capable of conducting flood, drought, and famine relief, the events

---

52. Khánh, *Vietnamese Communism*, p. 228.
53. Nørlund, "Rice and the Colonial Lobby," p. 207.
54. Gunn, *Rice Wars*, p. 117.

of the next decade would make it impossible to operate with such efficiency. The 1936-1937 crisis ended with a drop in rice prices in 1938.[55] Although this was partially due to an abundant harvest in Cochinchina, the fall in demand from China due to the beginning of the Second Sino-Japanese War also played a role. French Indochina's proximity to China meant that it was only a matter of time before the war reached Tonkin, whose land border with southern China was significant.

Tonkin and southern China were linked by the Hai Phong-Yunnan Railroad. During the beginning of the Second Sino-Japanese War, activity along the Hai Phong-Yunnan Railroad was allowed to continue, and revenue increased significantly during the war years (Tuan). This probably meant that the railroad was being used to transport goods to support the KMT across the Chinese border. After the French did not respond to Japanese requests to shut the railroad down, the Japanese began to bomb the railroad to put pressure on the French in 1939.[56] The Second World War had officially reached Vietnam, and with it came a variety of changes that would create the conditions for rapid change.

---

55. Ibid, p. 122.
56. Cam Anh Tuan, "The Hải Phòng-Yunnan Railway: An Important Knot in French Indochina-Japanese Relations during the Second World War," in *Vietnam-Indochina-Japan Relations during the Second World War: Documents and Interpretations*, ed. Masaya Shiraishi, Nguyễn Văn Khánh, and Bruce M. Lockhart (Waseda University Institute of Asia-Pacific Studies, 2017), p. 256.

1940: Imperial Japan's Entry into Indochina Comes to a Head

Beginning in 1940, Indochina was dominated by three major parties: the French, the Japanese and the ICP. Each party, especially the Japanese, fundamentally changed Indochina's economic and political scene, which brought about both revolution and disaster. The entry of the Japanese into Indochinese affairs was only cemented with the German defeat of France and the establishment of the Vichy government in the June of 1940.[57] The advent of a new, German-allied government in France made it easier for the Japanese to expand their interests in the region, as represented by the Japanese bombing of Hai Phong and the Battle of Lang Son on September 22, 1940.[58] A day after the bombing, the Japanese and French signed an agreement that would allow the Japanese use of the port of Hai Phong and garrisons in the Lang Son area.[59] This provided a strategic base for the Japanese to attack southern China and other parts of Southeast Asia.

---

57. Kiernan, *Viet Nam*, p. 376.
58. Nguyễn Văn Khánh, "Japanese Agricultural Policy toward Vietnam during World War II: Nature and Consequences," in *Vietnam-Indochina-Japan Relations during the Second World War: Documents and Interpretations*, ed. Masaya Shiraishi, Nguyễn Văn Khánh, and Bruce M. Lockhart (Waseda University Institute of Asia-Pacific Studies, 2017), p. 239.
59. Gunn, *Rice Wars*, p. 133.

Japanese advance on Lang Son in 1940[60]

Additionally, the Japanese military presence in Indochina allowed them to requisition provisions, especially rice, for their own troops. Although no requests were made by the Japanese, French Indochina exported 468,280 tons of rice to Japan.[61] This consisted of 25.9% of Japan's total rice import for the year.[62] In later years, the tons of rice exported to Japan, as well as the percent-

---

60. Unknown, *Japanese Advance to Lang Son*. 1940. https://upload.wikimedia.org/wikipedia/commons/b/bd/Japanese_advance_to_Lang_Son1940.jpg.
61. The Anh Nguyen. "Japanese Food Policies and the 1945 Great Famine in Indochina," in *Food Supplies and the Japanese Occupation in South-East Asia,* ed. Paul H. Kratsoka (Palgrave Macmillan UK, 2016), p. 210.
62. Khánh, "Japanese Agricultural Policy," p. 241.

age of Japan's total rice import, would increase as Japan gained control of the Indochinese economy. The relationship between the Japanese and Vichy governments would come to define the agricultural and economic policy that affected the lives of millions of Vietnamese.

The advent of the war had an especially large impact on the farmers of Cochinchina, whose livelihoods were more dependent on the global market. The drop in rice prices due to the fall in demand from China, combined with the high taxes collected by the French government and the high cost of living, led to economic hardships for the farmers of the Mekong Delta.[63] At this time, the ICP's network in Cochinchina was highly developed, even more than the Tonkin and Annam regional committees' networks. To the southern regional committee, the circumstances caused by the war, in particular by the threat of the Japanese-allied Thailand, were ripe for an armed insurrection.

The regional committee planned the revolution for November 22, 1940, and while the Seventh Plenum had decided to call off the uprising, the decision did not reach Cochinchina due to the arrest of the messenger.[64] The plan was discovered by the Surete, and the numerous attacks on various military bases ended with failure.[65] This led to the effective destruction of the ICP's net-

---

63. Sud Chonchirdsin, "The Indochinese Communist Party and the Nam Ky Uprising in Cochin China, November-December 1940," *South East Asia Research* 5, no. 3 (1997), pp. 272-273.
64. Ibid, p. 278.
65. Gunn, *Rice Wars*, p. 150.

work in southern Indochina, similar to the destruction of the ICP's network in Annam nearly a decade before.[66] High-level ICP members were executed, and thousands more were arrested whether or not they were involved in the mistakenly ordered uprising. In addition to wrecking the southern ICP network, this altered the balance of power between the northern and southern leaders within the party. Now, power lay in the hands of the northern and central Vietnamese leaders, which would change the course of the ICP's and Vietnamese history towards a different strategy of insurrection.

Nam Ky Uprising, 1940.[67]

---

66. Khánh, *Vietnamese Communism*, p. 253.
67. Unknown, *Cochinchina uprising (Nam Kỳ Khởi Nghĩa) against the French in Saigon, 1940*, 1940. https://www.flickr.com/photos/13476480@N07/44919600194.

1941: The Rice Accords and the Formation of the Viet Minh

If the events of 1940 introduced all of the major players vying for control of Vietnam during the Second World War, the events of 1941 established the paths they would take towards the climax of 1945. The decisions made by the Vichy French, the Japanese, and the ICP in 1941 founded the institutions and relationships that would come to define the following years.

The most important development in Vichy-Japanese relations took place in the first half of 1941, with the signing of the "Accord Commercial Franco-Japonaise" in Tokyo. This agreement effectively tied Indochina's economy to Japan. Many Japanese imports were free from tariffs and the complicated payment system was designed to fulfil Japan's wartime needs. It provided Japan with the total surplus of the rice and corn harvest, as well as rubber and minerals. The Japanese requested Governor General Decoux to sign an agreement about the exportation of 100 tons of rice from Saigon to Japan and the transportation of a million tons of rice for the Japanese military in one year, including the amount of rice to provide for ten thousand Japanese troops stationed in Indochina.[68]

In addition to exporting rice to Japan at tariff free rates using a complex payment system, the French government was also obliged to provide ten thousand

---

68. Gunn, *Rice Wars*, p. 134.

Japanese troops arriving in Saigon, 1941[69]

Japanese troops stationed within Indochina with provisions. Initially, the yearly export was set at one million tons of rice and corn.[70] This accord accelerated the exploitation of Indochinese farmers, especially those in regions where subsistence farming was the primary mode of food production.

In order to control the market in Cochinchina in advance of the exports, the French formed the Comité de direction pour le commerce et l'exportation des paddy, riz et dérivé.[71] The northern equivalent was the Directions des Services Economiques based in Hai Phong.

---

69. Japanese Army, *Japanese Troops Entering Saigon in 1941*, 1941.
70. Khánh, "Japanese Agricultural Policy," p. 239.
71. Gunn, *Rice Wars*, p. 134.

This tight control of the economy was typical of Vichy France, however, the control of Indochina's economy was exercised for the purpose of meeting Japanese demands.

These methods resulted in the Indochinese exportation of 854, 577 tons of rice to Japan, according to the Ministere de l'Information. According to the *Annuaire statistique de l'Indochine*, the total amount of rice exported was 583,323 tons.[72] Based on the lower number, Indochinese rice exports consisted of a quarter of Japan's total rice imports.[73] Due to the harsh demands, French authorities restricted the daily individual ration of paddy to 750 grams.[74] This was the beginning of French contribution to a food shortage that would begin to affect Tonkin as early as 1943.

At this point, the ICP recognized that the new political situation in Indochina offered them new opportunities to further their goals. By 1941, it was clear that the combination of French and Japanese dominion over Indochina would likely destroy its land and people before the ICP got the opportunity to carry out the bourgeoisie-democratic revolution. In order to deal with the new situation in Indochina, the ICP met at its Eighth Plenum in the caves of Pac Bo, on the Chinese border.[75]

Conducted in the mountainous homeland of the Nung ethnic minority, the famous Nguyen Ai Quoc (later Ho Chi Minh) presided over the meeting, which was

---

72. Nguyen, "Japanese Food Policies," p. 210.
73. Khánh, "Japanese Agricultural Policy," p. 241.
74. Nguyen, "Japanese Food Policies," p. 214.
75. Khánh, *Vietnamese Communism*, p. 257.

dominated by representatives from the north and central regions. The most important decision made at the plenum was the decision to temporarily put aside the bourgeoisie-democratic revolution and focus on the national liberation revolution.[76] By choosing to focus on national liberation, the ICP gained the ability to take advantage of Vietnamese nationalism and therefore obtain popular support, even from non-communists.

The formation of the League for the Independence of Vietnam, commonly known as the Viet Minh, was the key to obtaining this popular support. Based on the concept of the popular front, the Viet Minh front was technically an organizational front of the ICP, but this was disguised through the creation of "National Salvation" organizations that translated communist jargon into easily spreadable slogans for the common people, communist or not.[77] From 1941 onwards, the Viet Minh would serve as the ICP's primary organizational front.

1942: The Intensification of Agricultural Exploitation

As the Second World War raged on in Europe and Asia, French and Japanese exploitation of Indochina accelerated. 1942 saw the advent of various strategies implemented by the French in order to satisfy growing Japanese demands. These strategies would prove fatal as they were implemented, sowing the seeds of famine

---

76. Ibid, p. 260.
77. Ibid, p. 264.

in Tonkin. Two major agreements, which would deeply affect French policy towards Indochinese farmers, were made in 1942. The first of these was signed on July 18, in which the Vichy government agreed to provide the Japanese with 1,050,000 tons of rice and 45,000 tons of white flour.[78] The second was signed on August 19, which promised the Japanese the entire exportable surplus of rice from the 1942-1943 harvest.

In order to meet the numbers required by the Japanese, the Vichy government founded the Comite des Cereales, which operated through the Comptoir des Cereales.[79] This state-owned company maintained a monopoly over rice procurement, cutting out the traditional middlemen. However, the process by which the state collected its rice was far from beneficial to the farmers of Indochina. In Tonkin, 1942 saw the beginning of state requisition of rice.[80] The implemented system was based on land ownership. Essentially, villagers were forced to provide the state with a portion of their paddy proportional to the amount of land they owned.[81] The fixed price imposed by the government was much lower than the market price, leading to increased economic hardship.

In addition to requisitioning paddy, the French government began enforcing crop conversion in order to meet the imposed quotas of other goods such as cas-

---

78. Gunn, *Rice Wars*, p. 136.
79. Nguyen, "Japanese Food Policies," p. 209.
80. Khánh, "Japanese Agricultural Policy," p. 242.
81. Nguyen, "Japanese Food Policies," p. 212.

tor oil and jute.[82] Between 1941 and 1943, the acreage of land cultivated for fibrous and oleaginous plants increased by a factor of anywhere between three and fifteen.[83] The effect of the enforced cultivation of non-staple plants led to a fall in the amount of rice being produced, which contributed to the impending food crisis.

At the end of 1942, the French exported 973,000 tons of rice to Japan, which made up 37% of the total of Japan's imported rice. This did not meet Japan's initial request of 1,050,000 tons of rice, indicating that the Japanese demands were unrealistic.[84] This was true especially given the circumstances in which Indochinese farmers, especially Tonkinese farmers, were working. Tonkin's high, concentrated population, combined with the high paddy levies, enforced crop conversion, and high market price, led to worsening living conditions.

As the farmers suffered under the yoke of unrealistic Japanese and French rice quotas, the liberation front underwent a period of stagnation. In the latter half of 1941, the Vichy government destroyed the Viet Minh base in the northern, mountainous region of Bac Son, resulting in a lack of momentum in the Viet Minh's preparations for insurrection. Even Nguyen Ai Quoc, now using the name Ho Chi Minh, was imprisoned on a trip to China to gain KMT support for the Viet Minh's

---

82. Khánh, "Japanese Agricultural Policy," p. 243.
83. Bùi Minh Dũng, "Japan's Role in the Vietnamese Starvation of 1944-45," *Modern Asian Studies* 29, no. 3 (1995), p. 591.
84. Khánh, "Japanese Agricultural Policy," p. 241.

cause.[85] Overall, 1942 saw the intensification of Japanese and French oppression of Vietnamese farmers and rebels.

1943: The Portents of Famine

Globally, 1943 was a turning point of the Second World War. The Axis powers suffered major setbacks in North Africa, Italy, and China, changing the circumstances within Indochina. However, the power dynamic between Vichy France and Japan was shifting to favor the Japanese. With the Franco-Japanese Accord of January 25, 1943, the Japanese were able to commission 1,125,000 tons of rice from Indochina, a greater amount than the previous year.[86] The Mitsui Bussan Kaisha, the company responsible for handling rice exports from Indochina to Japan, exercised even greater control over the system than in the previous year. In September, the Mitsui Bussan Kaisha squeezed the yield premium system to command even more rice deliveries.[87] This led to increased Japanese control over the rice exports, foreshadowing the military control that Japan would eventually exercise in 1945.

In order to meet the increased numbers demanded by the Japanese, French authorities further decreased

---

85. Jean Lacouture, Peter Wiles, *Ho Chi Minh: A Political Biography* (United States: Random House, 1968), 78.
86. Khánh, "Japanese Agricultural Policy," p. 241.
87. Gunn, *Rice Wars*, p. 136.

the daily paddy ration to under 500 grams.[88] Meanwhile, productivity in Tonkin was steadily declining, falling by about ten kilograms of paddy per year. The combination of the low daily paddy ration, low productivity, and high demands led to the beginnings of famine in Tonkin in 1943. Based on the continuity of their exploitative practices, the French authorities were either unable or unwilling to take steps to handle the issue before it grew into a full-blown famine.

Since peasants were unable to purchase rice at the high market price because they were forced to sell their own paddy at a low price to the state owned comptoir, raising the government's prices may have provided some relief. However, the Vichy government only increased prices by 25% in 1943, which did virtually nothing to ease the hunger of the farmers.[89] Another solution would have been to transport rice from the more productive region of Cochinchina to Tonkin. However, the Japanese had commissioned the North-South Railroad in late 1942 to transport weapons and soldiers, so government authorities were unable to use it to transport much-needed rice to Tonkin.[90]

The Allied forces were well aware of the Japanese use of the North-South Railroad and other infrastructure in Indochina to support their troops across Asia. Technically, Indochina came under the jurisdiction of the Southeast Asian Command (SEAC), an Anglo-Ameri-

---

88. Nguyen, "Japanese Food Policies," p. 214.
89. Ibid, p. 212.
90. Khánh, "Japanese Agricultural Policy," p. 241.

can joint operation led by Lord Admiral Mountbatten. However, the Americans were generally distrustful of European intentions in regions where they held colonial possessions, so initial American action in Indochina was conducted independently of the British or the French.[91] During 1943, the Fourteenth Air Force, stationed in Kunming, began bombing the Japanese transport lines within and off the coast of Indochina. By the end of 1943, any attempt to use land infrastructure or shipping routes to transport rice from Cochinchina to Tonkin was at high risk of being bombed by American forces.[92]

With the help of harsh policies that harmed the farmers of Vietnam, the Vichy government was able to provide Japan with 1,023,471 tons of rice in 1943.[93] The amount of rice that was exported to Japan consisted of 58.3% of Japan's total rice imports for the year. The land allotted for jute production in Tonkin grew from 300 hectares in 1942 to 14,200 hectares in 1943, all at the expense of rice fields. Rice exports to Japan hit their peak in 1943, even as food availability between 1942 and 1944 fell by as much as 25% in certain provinces.[94] 1943 saw both the beginnings of famine and further integration into Japan's Greater East Asia Co-Prosperity Sphere,

---

91. Ronald H. Spector, *Advice and Support: The Early Years, 1941-1960* (Washington DC: Center of Military History, 1985), p. 28.
92. Huff, "Causes and consequences of the Great Vietnam Famine," p. 20.
93. Khánh, "Japanese Agricultural Policy," p. 241.
94. Huff, "Causes and consequences of the Great Vietnam Famine," p. 9.

foreshadowing the climactic political and agrarian developments of 1945.

As the beginnings of famine began to affect Tonkin, the Viet Minh began the process of building their popular front. In February 1943, the ICP's Central Committee met to build a plan to accelerate preparations for insurrection.[95] The Central Committee recognized that they lacked support in the most crucial places since the Viet Minh had been unable to shed their worker-peasant character for a national character that would appeal to a greater sector of the population. Therefore, 1943 saw an increase in efforts to gain Viet Minh support among the rural and urban population. The Viet Minh's most important strategy during 1943 was to utilize the existing structures of Vietnamese society to gain support from the urban population (Khánh 273).[96] Although Viet Minh support had not yet reached its peak, support from city dwellers became crucial during the August Revolution of 1945, proving the importance of the Viet Minh's united front strategy.

At this point, the main Viet Minh base remained in the mountains of Cao Bang. In 1943, the Viet Minh claimed over 1,184 militiamen, 5,435 members, and several counties within the three northern provinces of Cao Bang, Lang Son, and Bac Kan.[97] This liberated base region proved resilient, even after the Vichy government began to target Viet Minh activities in the region in November 1943.

---

95. Khánh, *Vietnamese Communism*, p. 272.
96. Ibid, p. 273.
97. Ibid, p. 276.

Vo Nguyen Giap with a Viet Minh militia, 1944.[98]

The events of the years between 1940 and 1944 were the foundation for the Great Famine of 1944-1945. The advent of the Second World War led to Vietnam's domination by two colonial powers instead of one, placing Vietnam on the path to disaster. Four years of the enforced requisition of paddy and crop conversion pushed the Vietnamese people to the brink of starvation, especially in the densely populated region of Tonkin. However, leaders of the resistance movement saw the Second World War as an opportunity to escalate the fight for sovereignty over Vietnam. These four years brought the simmering tensions between the

---

98. Hoàng Văn Đức, *Vo Nguyen Giap, Vietminh forces, 1944*, 1944, https://commons.wikimedia.org/wiki/File:Vo_Nguyen_Giap,_Vietminh_forces,_1944.jpg.

Vietnamese, French, and Japanese to the boil, setting the stage for when these tensions would explode into violence and death in 1944 and 1945.

The Famine (1944-45)

Although the event historically recognized as the North Vietnam famine took place between 1944 and 1945, the onset of this atrocity had been set in motion decades prior under the French colonial mishandling of Vietnamese lands. In 1945, during the height of the famine, the Vietnamese agronomist Nghiem Xuan Yem published an article entitled "The Crisis of a Hungry Population," writing:

"*All through the sixty years of French colonization our people have always been hungry* [original italics]. They were not hungry to the degree that they had to starve in such numbers that their corpses were thrown up in piles as they are now. But they have always been hungry, so hungry that their bodies were scrawny and stunted, so hungry that no sooner had they finished with one meal than they started worrying about the next; and so hungry that the whole population had not a moment of free time to think of anything besides the problem of survival."[99]

Rice output in Tonkin had been falling for decades, but its population was growing. As early as the 1920s, Tonkin was teetering on the precipice of food insecurity,

---

99. Vĩnh Long Ngô, *Before the Revolution: The Vietnamese Peasants Under the French* (Cambridge, Mass: MIT Press, 1973), p. 122.

A mass of hungry citizens begging in front of a market in Hanoi.[100]

consuming around eighty percent of the food grown in its region, whereas Cochinchina consistently maintained a surplus. The poor in Tonkin often only ate a single meal per day and were only sufficiently fed for about four months out of the year, typically after harvests. The specter of famine always loomed—in 1937, it was narrowly avoided only by rice imports from Cochinchina's surplus.[101] Sugata Bose pinpoints 1943 as the year when

---

100. Vo An Ninh, *Famine in Vietnam, 1945*, 1945, Museum of Vietnamese History, Hanoi, http://www.thanhniennews.com/arts-culture/horrific-photos-recall-vietnamese-famine-of-1945-37591.html.
101. Huff, 'Causes and consequences of the Great Vietnam Famine', p. 289.

starvation deaths began *en masse* in Tonkin,[102] but the worst phase lasted from May 1944 until March 1945.

The years 1941-44 saw the conversion of an unspecified quantity of Tonkin rice land to industrial crops such as jute and castor oil seed. Natural crises added another layer of hardship—drought and insects decreased the spring 1944 rice harvest by nineteen percent compared to the spring 1943 crop, and on top of it all, a string of typhoons ruined the rice crop that would have been harvested in the autumn of 1944. Tonkin farmers were forced to sell much of what little viable rice was left over to the colonial government, leaving them with nothing to feed themselves or their families.[103]

By December 1944, many peasants in Tonkin and northern Annam were forced to subsist on anything that was available: rice husks, banana tree roots, clover, and tree bark. Most Tonkin peasants had typically relied on purchasing imported clothing, as Vietnam produced very little of its own textiles, but Japan had sent almost none after the onset of World War II. Combined with the particularly cold winter that year, a large number of rural Tonkinites tried to escape to larger towns and cities where there might have been more available resources, but many died on the journey.[104]

---

102. Sugata Bose, "Starvation Amidst Plenty: The Making of Famine in Bengal, Honan and Tonkin, 1942-45," *Modern Asian Studies* 24, no. 4 (1990), p. 701.

103. Marr, *Vietnam 1945*, p. 96.

104. Huff, 'Causes and consequences of the Great Vietnam Famine', p. 292.

Famine victims in Hanoi, 1945.[105]

The number of casualties from the famine came to a zenith during the spring of 1945 that preceded the June rice harvest. Amid this, on March 9 the French colonial government encountered a *coup de force* by the

---

105. Vo An Ninh, *Famine in Vietnam, 1945*, ibid.

Japanese, who feared a French colonial uprising against them as their power in the war waned. French general Charles de Gaulle, leader of the Free France movement against the Nazi government in World War II, had hoped against, but still anticipated, a challenge to the Indochina colonial administration. However, de Gaulle wound up attempting to employ the coup to gain political power, as this Franco-Japanese tension proved that the Nazi-collaborating Vichy France state had truly fallen, shielding French resistance fighters from residual Allied criticisms.[106] On March 24, de Gaulle issued a declaration of condemnation about the coup, attempting to assure the people of Indochina that France was fighting for them—that they stood in solidarity.[107]

However, on the other side, Imperial Japan had quickly announced their seizure of power, and the Vietnamese were reveling in France's public humiliation.[108] Japan promised to support Vietnamese moves towards autonomy, and even actively encouraged Vietnamese emperor Bảo Đại to declare independence, but left the details of what 'independence' entailed vague.[109]

Although the worst waves of the famine were subsiding by August 1945, when the Viet Minh took over and established the Democratic Republic of Vietnam, the north's food supply was once again threatened by natural disaster. Several breaks in the Red River's dikes flooded

---

106. Marr, *Vietnam 1945*, p. 327.
107. Ibid.
108. Ibid, p. 109.
109. Ibid, p. 114.

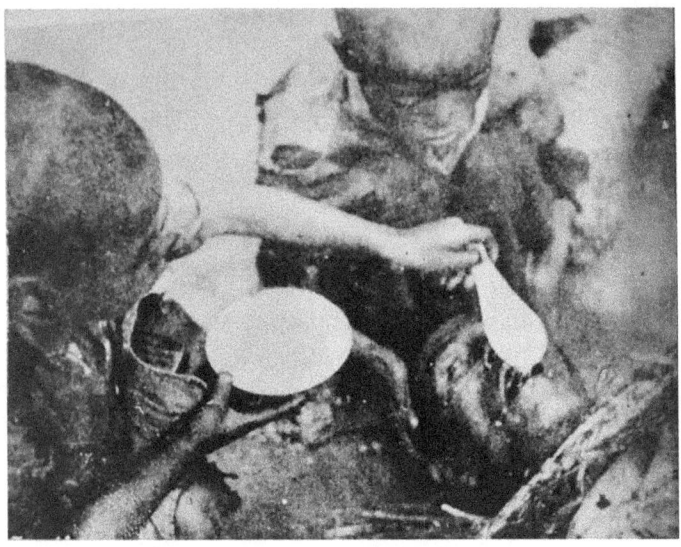

Vietnamese children pouring rice porridge into the mouth of their father.[110]

more than 300,000 hectares of rice fields, resulting in a loss of about one-third of the crop that would have been harvested in November.[111] A large-scale emergency response began quickly, as the nascent government of the establishing Democratic Republic of Vietnam faced an early leadership test in their ability to rehabilitate the dike system and stymie the numbers of starvation casualties. A successful campaign to grow corn, yams, and beans to mitigate the effects of the lost rice reflected positively on their ability to govern but could not fully compensate for the region's losses. Additional measures

---

110. Vo An Ninh, *Famine in Vietnam, 1945*, ibid.
111. Ibid, p. 508.

were taken to transport some of the south's rice surplus to the suffering north. Revolutionary committees developed militaristic defense plots to protect ships carrying rice northward, but they were met with bureaucratic obstacles, largely caused by French officials refusing to aid or defer to Vietnamese jurisdiction. Although relief efforts continued, confidential Democratic Republic of Vietnam records recorded at least 11,458 deaths from starvation as a result of the August floods.[112]

It was not until June 1946 that the threat of mass famine began to dissipate, aided by good weather and a plentiful summer harvest. Finally, in November 1946, the north enjoyed a bountiful rice crop and the danger of mass famine had all but vanished.[113]

Opinions about the primary cause of the famine vary among historians, however, it is universally agreed that a triumvirate of consequences from French colonization, Japanese imperialism, and natural disaster combined to make the famine the catastrophe that it was. The next chapter will examine the different influences and their impact on the famine, as well as the legacy that the famine left on Vietnam and its people and how it is studied and remembered today.

---

112. Ibid, p. 509.
113. Huff, 'Vietnam and Java Famines,' p. 644.

Examining the Causes and Influences that Led to the Famine

Geography

It is important to understand some of the geographical context of the famine and the way it was distributed. There was a clear disparity between the rural areas' experience of the famine and that of the cities and towns—Tonkin and northern Annam's rural villagers felt the famine 'earlier and more severely' than those in larger areas.[114] The drops in harvest output from 1942-1944 were highly localized. These drops were concentrated in eight coastal provinces, five in the Tonkin delta and three in North Annam. These provinces were not necessarily the most densely populated, but according to Huff, the existence of a strong correlation between drops in output and coastal provinces are indicative of the significance of natural disasters in cat-

---

114. Marr, *Vietnam 1945*, p. 101.

alyzing the famine.[115] The crops of the coastal provinces were afflicted with typhoons, a tidal wave, and floods, and Huff posits that famine might have been avoided or assuaged had these crops not been damaged.[116]

However, the geographic distribution of the viable rice that was harvested also played a role. Requisitions from the French and Japanese were disproportionately distributed to people in Vietnam's larger cities. A meager amount of rice was rationed out to residents, but much of it was stockpiled by the French and Japanese for their own potential emergency use in the future.[117] Marr suggests that Tonkin's 1944 output of 1.68 million tons of paddy, if fairly distributed, would have provided each of its 9,851,000 residents with 171 kilograms of rice, which might have been enough sustenance to survive until the June 1945 harvest.[118] Instead, rural villagers were largely left to their own devices. The levy rice that the French collected during their regime was largely distributed to cities, which Huff directly states as a reason why urbanites' experience of the famine was ameliorated compared to their rural counterparts.[119]

Even after the March 9 coup, when Japanese officials distributed some of the paddy from captured French stockpiles, the majority of it was allocated to residents

---

115. Huff, 'Vietnam and Java Famines,' p. 630.
116. Ibid.
117. Marr, *Vietnam 1945*, p. 101.
118. Ibid, p. 97.
119. Huff, 'Vietnam and Java Famines,' p. 646.

of urban areas.[120] The Japanese takeover overturned a French policy blocking access to the major urban areas of Hanoi and Haiphong, leading to the abandonment of many police barricades at city entrances. This greatly increased the flow of destitute rural villagers—at least, those who had survived this far—who had heard legends of abundance in areas outside of their villages.[121] They would wander main roads, begging for aid, but were given little, even from the more privileged Vietnamese. Author Tran Van Mai documented facets of this disparity, writing about the experience of attending an urban market during Tet (the Lunar New Year) at the height of the famine:

> "The customers in the wine shop talked about the New Year market and about starvation. To season their tales, they drank several cups of wine apiece to go with their ham, boiled chicken, roast pork, or hot bowls of noodle soup… They conversed in deep measured tones and laughed happily. Meanwhile, the hungry, who had risked their lives robbing food in the market, were being dragged back to this same area and were there tied up with their arms twisted behind them around the pillars of the shop. Now and then a customer would stand up and point a finger at them, yelling insults; 'The

---

120. Marr, *Vietnam 1945*, p. 101.
121. Huff, 'Vietnam and Java Famines,' p. 646.

best thing to do would be to have you bums beaten to death.'"[122]

About the Allocation of Blame

There is no single, simple explanation for why the famine happened, or why it reached the levels of devastation that it did. According to Gunn, the Japanese shredded documents to avoid blame, and the French official records went 'blank' after the Japanese coup.[123] One of the few firsthand Vietnamese perspectives on the famine that has been translated into English comes from Tran Van Mai, who calls the causes 'deep and complicated.' In his account, he presents an objective perspective on the event, but says that he believes 'these things will suffice for the reader to judge for himself the total situation.'[124]

When Ho Chi Minh proclaimed the independence of the Democratic Republic of Vietnam (DRV) in September 1945, he cited both French and Japanese actions directly, stating: "From [1940] our people were subjected to the double yoke of the French and the Japanese. Their sufferings and miseries increased. The result was that from the end of last year to the beginning of this year, from Quang Tri province to the North of Viet-

---

122. Long, *Before the Revolution*, pp. 234-35.
123. Gunn, *Rice Wars*, p. 246.
124. Long, *Before the Revolution*, p. 221.

nam, more than two million of our fellow-citizens died from starvation."[125]

However, Marr (an American historian who served in the U.S. Marine Corps during the Vietnam War) believes that survivors of disasters such as famine want to allocate blame[126] and names French colonial authorities as the primary targets of Vietnamese ire. There is substantial evidence to corroborate Marr's claim here. For example, Mai, writing in 1956, states that the French had used 'scientific methods' to create a devastating famine in order to ensure that the Vietnamese people could not revolt, as they had witnessed growing national liberation movements and increased pressure from Japanese imperial authorities, and felt their position in Indochina was compromised.[127] Long, translating Mai in the 1970s, says that this was the perspective of most Vietnamese, even at the time of his writing. However, he adds the caveat that historical evidence shows that the French were uncertain of their own future and took precautionary measures, such as rice hoarding, to protect themselves. While he does not deny the role this played in creating the famine, he seems to dispel the notion that it was a meticulously calculated plan on their part. Additionally, a few months after declaring DRV independence, Minh published an article in the Viet Minh periodical *Báo Cứu Quốc* that pinned starva-

---

125. Ho Chi Minh, *Selected Works Vol. 3*. (Hanoi: Foreign Languages Publishing House, 1960-62).
126. Marr, *Vietnam 1945*, p. 106.
127. Long, *Before the Revolution*, p. 221.

tion on the French, writing (in Vietnamese): "Because of the cruel policies of the French colonialists, such as forcing the harvest of rice, forcing the cultivation of jute, etc., in the first few months of this year more than two million compatriots in the North died of starvation."[128]

Pieces of this narrative seem to persist in contemporary Vietnam. A 2019 article published in the Vietnam law periodical *Pháp luật* outlines the influence of Japanese occupation and natural disasters on the famine in addition to French colonialism, but ultimately seems to place the brunt of the blame on the French.[129] The article ends with a condemnation of the French colonists' reported denial of their responsibility for the famine. According to Anh, French colonists claimed that there remained enough rice to prevent widespread hunger until the March 9 Japanese coup. The French government claimed to be 'determined to take strict measures against speculative activities with the intention of keeping the granaries to sell to the people to prevent the price of rice from skyrocketing,' but that the coup had prevented that intention from coming to fruition.[130]

---

128. Ho Chi Minh, "Visiting Professor Lectures on Photographer," Hô Hào Nhân Dân Chống Nạn Đói [Exhorting the People to Fight Hunger]," *Báo Cứu Quốc* [National Salvation Newspaper], (Hanoi), Nov. 8, 1945.
129. Minh Anh, "Nguồn cơn nạn đói kinh hoàng khiến gần 2 triệu người chết năm Ất Dậu," *Bao Phap Luat*, 12 December 2019, https://baophapluat.vn/nguon-con-nan-doi-kinh-hoang-khien-gan-2-trieu-nguoi-chet-nam-at-dau-post325700.html.
130. Ibid.

There seems to be little to no evidence that this claim was effective at redirecting Vietnamese ire. The author of an article published in the April 28, 1945 issue of the Hanoi periodical *Viet-Nam Tan Bao* had this to write:

> "When we passed through areas that had once seen rice and potatoes growing in abundance and had been thriving with activity, all we could see now were dry paddy fields and people who were weak and tired. Why was there this desolation? Because no sooner did the population grow the crops than the government took most of it away. Because the population had been so hungry that their strength had wasted away and they could not continue working."[131]

In contrast, Marr notes that the Japanese have historically received much less vilification, which he attributes to the fact that people knew the French had administrative control for the vast majority of the famine's onset.[132] He additionally theorizes that Japan's culpability may have been ameliorated by the highly-publicized grants of grain to famine victims after the coup. Vietnam's Emperor Bảo Đại and his cabinet, established on April 17, 1945, also evaded condemnation, as they were perceived to be fairly weak against colonial and imperial forces, however, they did receive some credit

---

131. Long, *Before the Revolution*, p. 132.
132. Marr, *Vietnam 1945*, p. 106.

for attempting to end the Japanese system of obligatory rice sales early in the summer.[133]

Mai is correct, though, in stating the complexity of the causes that led to the famine—some factors played a larger role than others, but each is worth a nuanced examination. The subsequent sections of this chapter aim to provide that.

About the Impact of Natural Disasters and Agricultural Fallout

There is no denying that uncontrollable forces, including the aforementioned poor weather and natural disasters, aided in creating the conditions for the famine and its mass casualties. However, historians seem to be in unanimous agreement that governments could have largely—perhaps even entirely—prevented the catastrophe. For this reason, it is more worthwhile to focus on the steps taken (or lack thereof) by people who could have taken action.

The French Role in the Famine

As mentioned previously, the French colonial regime had shouldered much of the blame for the famine. Northern Vietnamese peasants never had plentiful

---

133. Ibid.

quantities of food under the colonial administration, and regardless of their direct actions during the 1944-45 period, many Vietnamese people apportioned blame to them due to the effects of their colonial regime that had created the conditions for the famine to occur in the first place.

The geographical circumstances of the region meant that Vietnam maintained a delicate balance of food supply, with the north often relied on imports from the bountiful south.[134] However, food scarcity did not always result in famine—amid the 1936-37 agrarian crisis, the French government had actively aided the northern Vietnamese in staving off famine by mobilizing rice shipments from Cochinchina.[135] At this point, Tonkin's provincial government saw the potential for famine as a persistent danger and devised a plan for "Création des offices de l'alimentation indigène [Creation of indigenous food offices]", which would have enabled the region to stockpile rice and fortified comprehensive relief measures. However, it was shut down by French colonial officials, who claimed that rice could always be transported to the north by rail if a truly dire situation were to arise.[136]

This delicate balance—and the French government's willingness to help—was upset by World War II. Huff names four French actions that make them partially cul-

---

134. Huff, 'Vietnam and Java Famines', p. 627.
135. Huff, 'Causes and consequences,' p. 290, 303.
136. Huff, 'Vietnam and Java Famines', p. 644.

pable for the 1944-45 famine.[137] The first was a French ban on inter-provincial trade, which put a moratorium on the south-north rice shipments that had proven vital for the northern peasants' sustenance. The second was the imposition of a myriad of bureaucratic forms and restrictions on flows of rice, which further stifled the possibility of transporting rice to famine-affected areas. Third were the French regulations that stipulated 85 percent of rice cargo was to be sold at an official price, with only 15 percent at the disposal of junk owners. These conditions dissuaded junk owners from undertaking northbound voyages, which had become increasingly dangerous due to American bombs and mines.

During this time, the civilian economy in Vietnam had rapidly deteriorated, creating an environment where big landlords and wholesale grain merchants often worked in conjunction with corrupt government officials and black market operations were more prevalent than legal transactions.[138] The price of rice rose exponentially between 1943 and May 1945, and even secondary crops such as corn and yams became incredibly expensive or simply disappeared from the market altogether. For a working-class family in Hanoi, the first three months of 1945 saw a 373 percent increase in the cost of food and wages did not keep up in accordance. The last reason Huff posits is a 1944 increase in a rice levy that the French imposed on farmers, from

---

137. Ibid.
138. Marr, *Vietnam 1945*, p. 98.

130,000 tons in 1943 to 186,000.[139] In 1943, peasants in the south had already been forced to sell their surpluses to the French government[140] which exacerbated the consequences of the shortage that occurred during the rough winter of 1944-45. However, Huff admits that the levy's enforcement was questionable,[141] as the devastated civilian economy had made levy prices so low that peasants would have resisted delivering it, and the poor harvest would have made it difficult to collect on the levy. Even when they were aware of the famine, officials made no moves to lighten the burden on Vietnamese peasants, and they continued to leverage the colonial system against them. According to Marr, the system "still struck fear into the hearts of most subjects, causing them to obey rules even at grave personal cost."[142] Farmers who could not provide enough rice were forced to purchase it at the astronomical black-market price and sell it to the government for a nominal price or face the consequence of being sent to work on a forced labor project far from their home.

However, the French were not willing to let the blame lie solely with them. On September 12, 1945—only ten days after the DRV declared their independence—the French countered allegations of their responsibility for the 1945 famine by the way of broad-

---

139. Huff, 'Vietnam and Java Famines', p. 644.
140. Ibid, p. 629.
141. Ibid, p. 645.
142. Marr, *Vietnam 1945*, p. 97.

casts over their national radio.[143] They provided four major counterarguments: first, they stated that it had been under Japanese occupation that rice was massively requisitioned and stocks ran down. Second, they said that war had destroyed the transportation system that could have allowed fairer distribution of what rice the region possessed. Third, they blamed the Japanese push to plant jute, vanilla and peanuts for diminishing the area available for rice cultivation. Fourth, they argued that a Japanese pillage of large estates had caused a 200,000-ton deficit in the rice harvest of October 1944. They claimed that, up until the March 9 coup, they had worked "assiduously" to get rice to famine-afflicted Tonkin, but that under the duress of the military takeover, they could not be expected to complete the duties that had been delegated to the Japanese and nascent independent Vietnamese officials. They cited the fact that the famine reached a critical point in April 1945, after the coup, as evidence in their favor.

A postwar French report noted that after the deficit from the October 1944 harvest, the Vichy French administration had indeed built up reserve stocks in each province, but blamed the Japanese for drawing on these stocks for their own self-serving reasons.[144] It claimed that a threatened, weakening Japan had removed rice stocks and thrown them into the Mekong River. The French also turned blame onto the "provisional" DRV government, who they claim had hampered French

---

143. Gunn, *Rice Wars*, p. 247.
144. Ibid.

government assistance in Red River Delta regions and indeed aggravated disorder and social unrest.

While this may have at least helped to dissipate the belief that the famine was a political move intentionally fostered by the French, many Vietnamese people (and even non-Vietnamese scholars writing about the famine) continue to apportion blame to their apathy. As the Vietnamese-born author Huỳnh Kim Khánh writes, "The reactions of Vietnam's colonial leaders to the famine would have made cynics of the most politically innocent. For all its solicitude in courting the Vietnamese elite, the Decoux regime showed an unconcern verging on callous contempt for the Vietnamese as humans. It did nothing to help the famine victims."[145]

The truth, as it often does, seems to lie somewhere in the middle. French official Paul Chauvet comes closest out of all the recorded perspectives on the famine to find this middle ground, explaining that he regretted "the true nature of our preoccupations such as expressed by the heads of administrative services in not having been able to recognize earlier on and [even having] been privy through secondary considerations [the need to meet the shortfall in rice]," but continuing, "once the Indochina Council made the decision to quickly redress the penury of rice, then new attempts were made to achieve this goal."[146] In his analysis, Chauvet seems to own up to some of the administration's shortcomings, but still offloads the majority of

---

145. Khánh, *Vietnamese Communism*, p. 301.
146. Quoted in Gunn, *Rice Wars*, p. 248.

the blame onto others' shoulders in their unwillingness to accept or collaborate in French relief efforts, making it seem as though their complicity in the tragedy was more a matter of helplessness than the overt evil that they were often accused of.

Imperial Japan's Role

The Japanese government and military have historically received less blame for the famine due to the timing of their takeover. However, several historians believe that they had the capacity to do more to avoid (or at least lessen) the tragedy than the French and therefore, in their inaction, deserve more of the onus.

Even before the coup, notes Huff, the Japanese controlled rice exports and therefore had the power to manage decisions in Vietnam.[147] Since the early years of World War II, Japan had been shipping large quantities of Vietnamese rice to themselves, but this in and of itself had not created the famine. However, they had also forced the planting of non-rice crops in Tonkin and Annam to fulfill the needs of the Greater East Asia Co-Prosperity Sphere, which placed them at the center of a largely self-sufficient East and Southeast Asia. According to Huff,[148] if the land that had been used for non-rice crops between 1942 and 1944 had instead been used for rice, this could have produced 1,792 extra

---

147. Huff, 'Causes and consequences,' p. 304.
148. Ibid.

tons of rice in Annam and 18,600 tons in Tonkin. Of course, there is no guarantee that this much rice could or would have been harvested—these numbers represent the upper boundaries—and, even with such an addition, the famine might still have happened, but it nonetheless contributed to the tragedy.

Unlike many historical analyses of the famine, Bui Minh Dung squarely places the majority of the blame on the Japanese.[149] Dung argues the insignificance of many of the suggested causes, stating that the existence of multiple causes does not preclude the analysis of the relative impact each one had on the famine. First, he argues against the idea that a permanent subsistence crisis existed in the famine-afflicted regions, an idea that insinuates that even the slightest of worsened conditions would have killed the northern Vietnamese peasants, stating that if this were true, modern Vietnam would still be known for mass starvation. He then argues against the notion of bad weather as a foremost cause of the famine, which is what General Tsuchihashi Yuichi, who helmed the Japanese occupation army in 1944, claimed. The worst flooding and harvest came in the fall of 1945, after the famine had already peaked, demonstrating that weather was not, in fact, the determining factor in the people's survival. While Dung acquiesces that the French regime certainly contributed to the famine in their rice hoarding and contributions to the destruction of the civilian economy (though he

---

149. Bùi Minh Dũng, "Japan's Role in the Vietnamese Starvation of 1944-45," *Modern Asian Studies* 29, no. 3 (1995), pp. 573-586.

claims inflation actually hurt city dwellers, relatively few of whom suffered deaths from starvation, more than the rural peasants), he also states that they served as a check against Japanese 'excesses'. Lastly, he argues against the significance of Allied bombing, which damaged the transport systems that could have transported rice to the famine-afflicted north in exacerbating the famine. General Tsuchihashi named the "disintegration" of the system as one of the two main causes of the famine, however, the Japanese had continued using it "considerably" on the grounds of military precedence, proving that it could not have been as destroyed as Tsuchihashi claimed. Marr states that by early 1945, the Japanese were using two-thirds of all rail capacity for the sake of their military.[150]

Instead, Dung posits that the Japanese economic policies that served to benefit their status within the Greater East Asia Co-Prosperity Sphere, as well as their military actions "systematically played a role considerably greater" than any others.[151] Japanese officials believed that exploiting resources in French Indochina would be of economic benefit to their country, so they began importing supplies such as rice, raw cotton, rubber, vegetable oil, coal, and metal ores as early as the beginning of the twentieth century.[152] By the early 1940s, the Delegation of Foreign Ministry for the investigation of resources had turned their interest towards the poten-

---

150. Marr, *Vietnam 1945,* p. 100
151. Ibid, p. 618.
152. Ibid, p. 587.

tial of agroforestry resources, at which point extensive forced crop conversion policies were enacted. The Japanese had found Tonkin in particular to have great potential for growing crops that they desired, such as tung oil, jute, and hemp, and they forced Tonkinites to use much of what had been land for rice crops for these resources.

It has been reported that it was in fact French authorities who imposed this change of crops and that the changes were necessary for Indochinese consumption.[153] Dung refutes this, stating that crop conversion was decidedly not geared towards the needs of Tonkin's indigenous people and that the French were largely acting on the orders of the Japanese officials that had occupied the region. He also calls into question the assertions that the crop shifts had a marginal or unimportant effect on Vietnamese farmers. In 1943, the year the Japanese enforced crop conversion policies on a large scale, the area of rice cultivation in Tonkin was reduced from 1,487,000 hectares in 1941-42 to 1,386,000 hectares the next year.[154] The Japanese and French both forcibly collected and hoarded rice in military depots throughout 1944, which certainly played a role in Vietnamese peasants' food access, but it seems as though much of the rice collected served primarily to meet demands for rice exports to Japan. Dung even cites evidence that suggests the French might have used some of their agricultural organizations to protect both French and Vietnamese interests,[155] but there is lit-

---
153. Ibid, pp. 589-90.
154. Ibid, p. 592.
155. Ibid, p. 608.

tle evidence to provide any idea of the extent to which the French were actually looking out for the Vietnamese. However, it is fairly clear that the Japanese and French's motivations and priorities in rice and grain collection began to diverge after Vichy France fell, and Japan no longer appeared to be interested in collaborating with a liberated France.

Even after their March 9 coup, Imperial Japanese officials neglected to address the famine (which was quickly approaching emergency proportions) for at least two weeks, and when they did act, they mostly reaffirmed draconian French policies such as compulsory rice sales.[156] While they did release some grain from French depots that they had captured, perhaps as a strategic move to gain favor with the native population and keep up the appearance that they wanted to support Vietnamese independence, that grain was largely apportioned to urbanites and the Japanese continued the forcible extraction of rice through the worst of the famine and until their surrender in September 1945.

The Consequences and Aftermath

Despite Marr's belief that famine survivors sought to find someone to blame,[157] it is perhaps futile for historians, particularly Western academics, to focus scholarship on pointing fingers as opposed to studying the

---

156. Ibid, p. 101.
157. Ibid, p. 106.

Vietnamese perspective and the legacy the famine left on natives. A Vietnamese verse from the time of the famine, quoted by Khánh sums up this tension well:

Nhat cuoi, Tay khoc, Tau lo;
Viet Nam Doc lap chet co day duong.

(The Japanese laugh, the French weep, the Chinese worry; Independent Vietnamese curl up and die all over the streets.)[158]

As Khánh puts it, during the winter and spring of 1944-45, the French were nursing their political wounds, Japan was focused on their waning power amid growing anti-Japanese sentiment worldwide, and the small minority of educated Vietnamese in urban centers were hunting for power, as millions in rural areas were struggling for mere survival.[159]

Total Devastation: Statistics of the Estimated Deaths

In the DRV Declaration of Independence, Ho Chi Minh calculated that the 1944-45 famine resulted in 2 million deaths, and this figure was taken as fact by many at the time. However, in recent years, this number has come to be generally regarded as too high. One official report from the French Centre des Archives

---
158. Khánh, *Vietnamese Communism*, p. 301.
159. Ibid, p. 299.

d'Outre-Mer provides a figure of 1.3 million, however, Huff notes that there is no information on how the figure was derived.[160] Marr names a much lower number, around one million deaths, a 'more credible estimate.'[161] Regardless of this, the implications are atrocious: one million people was about 10% of Tonkin's population at the time. It would have been incredibly difficult, perhaps even impossible, to garner an accurate count of the death toll, as many people fled rural areas and died in or on the way to larger cities. By 1945 in Hanoi, famine victims were dying by the hundreds every single day. Facing a lack of land and time to care for each victim's body individually, survivors had to bury corpses *en masse* in shallow graves.

Moves Towards Independence and the Rise of the Viet Minh

The devastation caused by the famine played an undeniable role in paving the way for revolution and the Viet Minh's rise to power. In concert with the Japanese coup and weakened view of the French as they transitioned away from the Vichy administration, the Viet Minh was able to use the famine to their political advantage in that no other party or authority was offering alleviation from the suffering or a genuine path to independence. The famine was integral to the Vietnamese revolution

---

160. Huff, 'Vietnam and Java Famines,' p. 621.
161. Marr, *Vietnam 1945,* p. 104.

in that it created a 'sense of desperation' necessary to provide an opportunity to enrage—and subsequently mobilize—rural peasants.[162]

By early 1945, the French administration was well aware of the threat of the Viet Minh exploiting the crisis. In February 1945, the first recorded example of Viet Minh print propaganda popped up in the reading room of the Bibliotheque Pierre Pasquier, a call to action asking the student population to rise up.[163] Although they made attempts to dissipate the growing discontent in these early months before the Japanese coup, such as lessening paddy levies, relinquishing some of the area provided to the Japanese for forced crop cultivation, and attempting to stop further increases in the price of rice,[164] it was to little avail.

Meanwhile, the Japanese had shifted their alliance away from France after the Vichy administration fell and began collaborating with the Viet Minh, supplying them with—including some seized from the French after the coup—and even fighting alongside and cohabitating with indigenous Vietnamese.[165] However, the Viet Minh knew not to rely on the Japanese. Under the facade of encouraged independence, astute Vietnamese wondered if they were being given a chimera[166] as the unity between the Japanese and Vietnamese seemed to be contingent

---

162. Huff, 'Vietnam and Java Famines,' p. 651.
163. Gunn, *Rice Wars*, p. 190.
164. Ibid, p. 191.
165. Ibid, pp. 191-92.
166. Marr, *Vietnam 1945*, p. 115.

on loyalty to the hierarchical order, and rebellion would be 'severely punished in conformity with military discipline', according to a proclamation from General Tsuchihashi in April 1945.[167] Regardless of this, Vietnamese communists saw this time as their best opportunity to make strides towards independence and continued plotting their own agenda during the time between the March coup and the August Revolution.

Dung provides a clear example of their strategy in a recounting of their response to continued forcible rice extraction.[168] When a group of Japanese soldiers and Vietnamese 'security troops' employed by the Japanese came to the famine-afflicted Bac-Ninh province in July 1945 to ensure a transport of rice to the provincial capital, villagers rose up to blockade them, and a Viet Minh group was able to convince the security troops to side with their own and aid in defeating the Japanese. However, the provincial committee leader considered it unwise to allow the people to wipe out the Japanese soldiers and directed an unarmed demonstration.

We might surmise that this was a strategy to avoid suspicion from the Japanese, not allowing them to know truly how powerful and potentially dangerous the Viet Minh had become before they were ready for a large-scale attack. It was to their benefit to stay under the radar at this point, as Japan was largely preoccupied defending their position in the war, too busy to give much thought to Vietnamese activity. Khánh believes

---

167. Ibid.
168. Dung, 'Japan's Role,' pp. 615-16.

that the five months between the coup and revolution were 'the most important period' in the history of the party, and they were focused on expanding their influence among the populace and strengthening their forces.[169] Within three months of the coup, Viet Minh forces essentially controlled the mountain regions and executed guerrilla attacks on the Japanese—ambushing convoys, cutting roads, attacking military posts—until their eventual surrender. This garnered a positive and powerful reputation for the Viet Minh, giving them an air of political prestige as the sole Vietnamese political collective that dared to attack the Japanese.[170]

Their political mobilization, though, became even more powerful than their military forces during this time. More than anyone realized at the time, society in Tonkin and northern Annam had been irreparably disrupted by the famine, and their outrage towards the administrations who had imposed these conditions upon them and then refused them aid left them wide open to Viet Minh exhortations. More than anything else, though, Marr writes, "they wished to avoid yet another encounter with starvation later in the year, if necessary by taking matters into their own hands" (*Vietnam 1945*, 150).[171] Initially, the famine had hurt revolutionary mobilization, as some Viet Minh members also became victims in the name of trying to stay connected to the masses, and others began to neglect

---

169. Khánh, *Vietnamese Communism*, p. 309.
170. Ibid, p. 311.
171. Marr, *Vietnam 1945*, p. 150.

the party due to hunger. They realized quickly, though, the opportunity the famine gave them to give people political consciousness. As the famine was setting in during the late fall of 1944, the party began to release propaganda with the slogan "Destroy the granaries, solve the danger of the famine!"[172]

Ho Chi Minh with members of the American Office of Strategic Services, 1945.[173]

The Viet Minh's calls to oppose levy collections, to demand the distribution of grain stocks hoarded by the French and Japanese, or even to 'liberate' the grain them-

---

172. Khánh, *Vietnamese Communism,* p. 313.
173. The Office of Strategic Services (OSS) sent operatives to northern Vietnam in 1945, where they worked with the Viet Minh. U.S. Army, *Ho Chi Minh (third from left standing) and the OSS in 1945,* 1945, https://commons.wikimedia.org/wiki/File:Ho_Chi_Minh_(third_from_left_standing)_and_the_OSS_in_1945.jpg.

selves by force, were well-received by villagers between March and May 1945. Before they were able to build up their weapons stock and military force, the party encouraged the people to perform unarmed actions, such as painting propaganda on public buildings or organizing marches to call for immediate famine relief from the government. Some went as far as to carry out those forceful liberations of grain, breaking into rice stockpiles or violently compelling guards to provide them access to grain. While it is unknown exactly how much grain was liberated by the Viet Minh's actions, an 'urgent' June 12 message from the provincial chief to Hanoi that reported the pillaging of stockpiled paddy shows that it was enough to cause concern among the existing administration.[174] While not necessarily advertised as such, the famine also bolstered the Viet Minh's recruitment efforts in that many unemployed and otherwise destitute young men from famine-stricken areas and families saw joining the group as a guaranteed way to at least ensure themselves a daily ration of rice.[175]

A series of events early in August 1945 provided the Viet Minh with the opportunity to finally seize power in what would come to be known as the August Revolution. On August 6, the United States detonated an atomic bomb on Hiroshima. On August 8, the Soviet Union declared war on Japan. On August 10, Japan offered to surrender. When this news reached Vietnam on August 13, the Viet Minh called upon the Vietnam-

---

174. Marr, *Vietnam 1945,* pp. 208-209.
175. Ibid, p. 210.

ese people and those in the Vietnamese Liberation Army to attack the cities and areas of importance to Japan, block their ability to escape, and disarm them.[176] During the middle of the month, all of Vietnam seemed to be caught in political uproar. Demonstrations and rallies raged in urban areas, administrative centers, and provincial seats of power, and Viet Minh flags, propaganda, slogans, and songs became ubiquitous. Under these conditions, Khánh writes, "power simply fell into Viet Minh hands."[177] On August 30, Bảo Đại formally

The Viet Minh during the August Revolution.[178]

---

176. Khánh, *Vietnamese Communism*, p. 322.
177. Ibid, p. 324.
178. Unknown, *Viet Minh during August Revolution*, 1945, https://commons.wikimedia.org/wiki/File:Viet_Minh_during_August_Revolution.jpg.

abdicated and relinquished power to the Viet Minh, and only three days later came Ho Chi Minh's declaration of independence and the country's establishment as the Democratic Republic of Vietnam.

A year after the August Revolution, Vietnamese communist leader Truong Chinh directly accredited the campaign against the famine as the turning point for the Viet Minh's rise to power, writing:

"Hundreds of thousands of our people lay dying next to Japanese and French granaries which were filled to the top. At the time, the essential task was the leadership of the masses for armed attacks on the Japanese granaries and the French colonialists' plantations, stocking all kinds of agricultural products. The Communist and Viet Minh cadres did grasp and solve this problem, causing the vast masses, either organized or unorganized, to participate eagerly in the movement against the Japanese. The more they participated in these activities, the more they saw the hideous face of the enemy and felt their own strength. It was thanks precisely to the attacks against the granaries and the plantations that the national salvation movement developed in an effervescent way."[179] According to Khánh, the Viet Minh's detractors lacked the political vision and strategy that the party had, stating that even years later, many struggle to truly see the political implications of the famine and to comprehend just how Communists were able to turn the tragedy into

---

179. *Cach mang thang Tam*, 25, quoted in Khánh, *Vietnamese Communism*, p. 314.

a self-serving political instrument—while also ensuring that their people were fed.[180]

Conclusion: The Long-Term Effects and Legacy of the 1944-45 Vietnam Famine

Although the famine was irrefutably a massive tragedy, very little documentation or accounts of the famine and its casualties exist today, particularly outside of the Vietnamese language. There are no available statistics about the losses that individual provinces or towns suffered, much less any demographic breakdowns. Even having them, though, would never be enough to sufficiently measure the psychological effects that the famine had on survivors or their descendants. As Marr writes, "The sounds of lamentation among starving compatriots, the sight of bodies strewn alongside rural roads and hedges, or encountered each morning on city sidewalks, continued to haunt several generations in northern and north-central Vietnam."[181] Even without major historical coverage outside of Vietnam until recent years, this event clearly continued to scar the Vietnamese people for decades.

In the nearly eight decades since the famine, though, there have been several attempts to recover and learn as much about the event and its long-term effects. In what Gunn refers to as a "truth-seeking exercise," Japanese

---

180. Ibid, p. 315.
181. Marr, *Vietnam 1945*, p. 105.

scholar Futura Motoo collaborated with a Vietnamese research team between 1992 and 1995 to conduct a retrospective mortality analysis of the famine through household surveys and interviews conducted in northern Annam and Tonkin.[182] Through their research, they found that economic factors had sharply separated the fate of families, as land-owning peasants tended to mitigate the effects of the famine, while the death rate for landless peasants climbed as high as 53.3 percent.[183]

However, the collection of statistics can only provide so much understanding of the tragedy. Oral histories collected since 1945 have provided a clearer, harrowing perspective on the minutiae of life under the worst of the famine's conditions. For instance, Vietnamese poet Bang Ba Lan provides an eyewitness account in "Doi, Doi 'They starved, They starved]":

"Along all highways famished bodies moaned,
lying curled up in the sun, in dust and filth.
Amidst those rags the hollow eyes alone
still harbored sparks of soul soon to go out.
And day by day, toward cities, toward Hanoi
more corpses, yet more corpses dragged themselves,
bringing the trail of flies, the stench of smells,
then crumbled down along some street or lane.
At dawn you'd gingerly push your door ajar
To check if there was someone dead outside."[184]

---

182. Gunn, *Rice Wars*, p. 248.
183. Ibid.
184. Quoted in Marr, *Vietnam 1945*, p. 137.

Another eyewitness, Tran Van Mai, told a story of a young family in his village where the parents were forced to choose between saving themselves at the expense of their three beloved children, or slowly allowing all of them to waste away:

> "From that day on, the couple ate alone and no longer divided the food up for the children. The children, being so hungry, would charge in on their parents' table whenever the latter sat down to eat and would grab at the food. Mr. Vuoc would beat them off and drive them out into the streets, allowing them to come back only at night to sleep. Sometimes they would return home after having roamed around the village, so hungry and tired they could walk no further. However, even then, if there was any food around the house, their father would, to their dismay, have to tie them up at the house posts lest they cause any trouble."[185]

More contemporary eyewitness accounts demonstrate the ways experiencing the famine affected survivors throughout their lives, for instance, the story of Mrs. Nguyen Thi Sot, interviewed by Vietnamese publication *VnExpress* in 2015:

---

185. 'A father who abandoned his children', translated in Long, *Before the Revolution*, pp. 246-50.

"There were 8 people in my family, 5 of them died... I was only 17 years old that year, in my youth, but only skin and bones remained. Many people were starving their whole body, unable to distinguish between a woman and a man. People stole all the patched clothes on the body of a pregnant woman about to give birth in exchange for a piece of cake to eat."[186]

A study of the famine would inevitably call into question assumptions about human morality and behavior. Of course, one could ask how a person could decidedly chain their children up to prevent them from eating or steal clothes off of an expectant mother's body, but on the other hand, how could the authorities deprive people of enormous stockpiles of grain, and continue to do so as hundreds of thousands died before their eyes? How could urbanites watch rural villagers pour into the city and turn their noses up, rather than provide whatever aid they could?

There is an important but understated reason to ask these questions and study atrocities such as this famine, particularly outside of the Western world. Westernized education tends to teach a very unilateral perspective of the Western world in World War II, amplifying the heroic aspects and downplaying the crimes and casual-

---

186. Nhóm phóng viên [Reporters team], "Nạn Đói Năm 45 Trong Ký Ức Người Còn Sống [Famine Year 45 in the Memory of the Living]," *VnExpress*, 13 Jan. 2015, http://vnexpress.net/nan-doi-nam-45-trong-ky-uc-nguoi-con-song-3130491.html.

ties. However, as these countries, particularly European imperialist powers, nursed their political and militaristic wounds, many nations across Africa and Asia seized the opportunity to build decolonial movements. Weakened European powers, lacking wealth and political clout, could do little to suppress nationalist uprisings happening continents away. This era of mass decolonization tends to be a mere paragraph or so in Western history textbooks, leaving the majority of the population generally ignorant about the movement. By ignoring the horrific ramifications of imperialism and colonization before and during (and even after) World War II, we lack the understanding of the legacies they left that continue to haunt the victims of such atrocities and their descendants. Such Eurocentric histories also help in creating conditions that prevent future historians, especially those with a Westernized education, from thinking critically about events, and subsequently from ever fully rectifying historical wrongs.

Nevertheless, there is also a very practical, pressing need to ask these questions, to remember the history of this famine—as recently as 1988, Hanoi sought emergency aid for acute rice shortages "in many localities" and starvation in the former Ha Son Binh province, which was in northern Vietnam (Crossette, 'Hanoi Seeks Emergency Aid').[187] According to Crossette, the Vietnamese press and radio reports at the time blamed weather conditions, depleted soil, and political and

---

187. Barbara Crossettes, "Hanoi, Citing Famine Fears, Seeks Emergency Aid," *The New York Times*, May 15. 1988.

economic mismanagement for the food crisis. Crossette also claims that there was evidence that people in the rice-growing areas of the south were hoarding rice instead of selling it. In response, the United States reportedly claimed that they were 'skeptical' of famine reports from Vietnam, as they believed them to be veiled requests for unnecessary aid.

Luckily, by 1990, the country had transformed its agricultural system. Toward the end of the twentieth century, Vietnam became one of the largest rice exporters in the world.[188] However, the fact that the region came so close to another agrarian devastation at the hands of almost the same causes that left a million people dead just 40 years before reveals the overtly dangerous possibility of historical tragedies repeating themselves when they go largely unreported. Acknowledging atrocities and understanding their causes, course, and effects is the key to both respecting atrocity victims and preparing for the future. As climate change and an increasingly tense political climate continue to plague nations once ravaged by imperialism and colonialism, understanding events like the Vietnam Famine of 1944-1945 is crucial in deepening the current understanding of the multiple causes of atrocities in order to prevent them in the future.

---

188. Keith B. Richburg, 'Near Famine in '88, Vietnam Now Exports Rice,' *The Washington Post*, April 19, 1990.

Bibliography

Primary Sources

Bàng, Bá Lân "Đói, đói" [They Starved, They Starved]. Translated by Hyunh Sang Thong. *Vietnam Forum* 5, 1985: 101-107.

Crossette, Barbara. "Hanoi, Citing Famine Fears, Seeks Emergency Aid." *New York Times*, May 15, 1988. https://www.nytimes.com/1988/05/15/world/hanoi-citing-famine-fears-seeks-emergency-aid.html.

Đảng Cộng sản Việt Nam. Lịch sử biên niên Đảng Cộng sản Việt Nam—Tập II [Vietnam Communist Party annual yearbook—Vol. 2]. Hà Nội: Nhà Xuất Bản Chính Trị Quốc Gia, 2008.

Du, Phan. "Hai Chau Lan To Tam" [Two Pots of Orchids]. Saigon: Cao Thom, 1965. http://www.tusachtiengviet.com/images/file/sqFEamUu0wgQAOJ3/sachviet-edu-vn.pdf.

Ho, Chi Minh. "Hô Hào Nhân Dân Chống Nạn Đói [Exhorting the People to Fight Hunger]." *Báo Cứu Quốc* [National Salvation Newspaper], November 8. 1945.

Ho Chi Minh. *Selected Works Vol. 3*. Hanoi: Foreign Languages Publishing House, 1962.

Mai, Tran Van. "Ai Gay Nen Toi?" [Who Committed This Crime?]. Saigon, 1956.

Nguyen, Ai Quoc. "Revendications du Peuple Annamite." 1919. http://vietnamwar.lib.umb.edu/origins/docs/Lansing.html.

Nhóm phóng viên [Reporters team]. "Nạn Đói Năm 45 Trong Ký Ức Người Còn Sống [Famine Year 45 in the Memory of the Living]." *VnExpress*, 13 Jan. 2015, www.vnexpress.net/nan-doi-nam-45-trong-ky-uc-nguoi-con-song-3130491.html.

Phuong, Hoang, and Phuong Hanh. "Hàng Chục Nghìn Người Đói Kéo Về Hà Nội Năm 1945 [Tens of Thousands of Hungry People Flocked to Hanoi in 1945]." *VnExpress*, 14 Jan. 2015, www.vnexpress.net/hang-chuc-nghin-nguoi-doi-keo-ve-ha-noi-nam-1945-3131438.html.

"Report on French Indo China from HQ SACSEA Commission No. 1, Saigon, 0800108139." Vietnam Center and Sam Johnson Vietnam Archive. 30 November 1945, Box 01, Folder 08, Peter Dunn Collection, Vietnam Center and Sam Johnson Vietnam Archive, Texas Tech University, https://www.vietnam.ttu.edu/virtualarchive/items.php?item=0800108139.

Vũ Khiêu. *Truy điệu những lương dân chết đói* [Commemorating good people who starved to death]. Báo Nhân Dân, 1945. http://tuoitre.vn/tin/chinh-tri-xa-hoi/20050318/truy-dieu-nhung-luong-danchet-doi/70864.html.

Yem, Nghiem Xuan. "Nan dan doi" [The Starvation Crisis of the People]. *Thanh Nghi,* no. 107 (May 5, 1945): 18.

Secondary Sources

Anh, Minh. "Nguồn cơn nạn đói kinh hoàng khiến gần 2 triệu người chết năm Ất Dậu." *Bao Phap Luat,* December 12, 2019, https://baophapluat.vn/nguon-con-nan-doi-kinh-hoang-khien-gan-2-trieu-nguoi-chet-nam-at-dau-post325700.html.

Bernal, Martin. "The Nghe-Tinh Soviet Movement 1930-1931." *Past & Present,* no. 92 (1981): 148-168.

Boissarie, Delphine. "Indochina During World War II: An Economy Under Japanese Control." In *Economies Under Occupation: The Hegemony of Nazi Germany and Imperial Japan in World War II,* edited by Marcel Boldorf and Tetsuji Okazaki. United Kingdom, Taylor & Francis, 2015.

Bose, Sugata. "Starvation Amidst Plenty: The Making of Famine in Bengal, Honan and Tonkin, 1942-45." *Modern Asian Studies* 24, no. 4 (1990): 699-727.

Chonchirdsin, Sud. "The Indochinese Communist Party and the Nam Ky Uprising in Cochin China, November-December 1940." *South East Asia Research* 5, no. 3 (1997): 269-293.

Cotter, Michael G. "Towards a Social History of the Vietnamese Southward Movement." *Journal of Southeast Asian History,* vol. 9, no. 1, 1968, pp. 12-24., doi: 10.1017/S0217781100003598.

Duiker, William J. *Ho Chi Minh: A Life*. United Kingdom: Hachette Books, 2000.

Dũng, Bùi Minh. "Japan's Role in the Vietnamese Starvation of 1944-45." *Modern Asian Studies* 29, no. 3 (1995): 573-618. Accessed July 30, 2021. http://www.jstor.org/stable/312870.

Furata, Motoo. "A Survey of Village Conditions during the 1945 Famine in Vietnam." In *Food Supplies and the Japanese Occupation in South-East Asia*, edited by Paul H. Kratsoka, Palgrave Macmillan UK, 2016, pp. 9-31.

Gunn, Geoffrey C. *Rice Wars in Colonial Vietnam: The Great Famine and the Viet Minh Road to Power*. Lanham, Maryland: Rowman & Littlefield, 2014.

Guven, Cahit, Trung Hoang, Muhammad H. Rahman, and Mehmet A. Ulubaşoğlu. "Long-term Effects of Malnutrition on Early-life Famine Survivors and Their Offspring: New Evidence from the Great Vietnam Famine 1944-45." *Health Economics* 30, no. 7 (2021): 1600-1627.

Hoàng, Văn Đức. *Vo Nguyen Giap, Vietminh forces, 1944*. 1944. https://commons.wikimedia.org/wiki/File:Vo_Nguyen_Giap,_Vietminh_forces,_1944.jpg.

Huff, Gregg. "Causes and Consequences of the Great Vietnam Famine, 1944-5." *The Economic History Review* 72, no. 1 (2019): 286-316.

—. "The Great Second World War Vietnam and Java Famines." *Modern Asian Studies* 54, no. 2 (2020): 618-653.

Huỳnh, Kim Khánh. *Vietnamese Communism, 1925-1945*. Ithaca: Cornell University Press, 1982.

Hurley, M. M., Minh, L. D., Sterling, E. J. *Vietnam: A Natural History*. Ukraine: Yale University Press, 2008.

Japanese Army. *Japanese Troops Entering Saigon in 1941*. 1941.

Khánh, Nguyễn Văn. "Japanese Agricultural Policy toward Vietnam during World War II: Nature and Consequences." In *Vietnam-Indochina-Japan Relations during the Second World War: Documents and Interpretations*, edited by Masaya Shiraishi, Nguyễn Văn Khánh, and Bruce M. Lockhart, 239-250. Waseda University Institute of Asia-Pacific Studies, 2017.

Kiernan, Ben. *Viet Nam: A History from Earliest Times to the Present*. New York: Oxford University Press, 2017.

Kratsoka, Paul H. "The Impact of the Second World War on Commercial Rice Production in South-East Asia." In *Food Supplies and the Japanese Occupation in South-East Asia*, edited by Paul H. Kratsoka, Palgrave Macmillan UK, 2016, pp. 9-31.

Lacouture, Jean, Wiles, Peter. *Ho Chi Minh; a Political Biography*. United States: Random House, 1968.

Laffey, John F. "Land, Labor and Law in Colonial Tonkin Before 1914." *Historical Reflections / Réflexions Historiques*, vol. 2, no. 2 (1976): 223-263. www.jstor.org/stable/41298668.

Le Coq, J. F., M. Dufumier and G. Trébuil. "History of rice production in the Mekong Delta." The Third Euroseas Conference, London, 2001.

La Lutte. 23 February 1935. 1935.

Lessard, Thomas. "The Vietnamese Famine of 1944-1945: Implications for the Rise of the Viet-Minh and Anti-Imperialism in French Indochina." Interdisciplinary Conference on Human Rights.

Li, Tana. "A Historical Sketch of the Landscape of the Red River Delta." *Trans-regional and -national Studies of Southeast Asia* 4, no. 2 (2016): 351-363.

MacLean, Ken. "History Reformatted: Vietnam's Great Famine (1944-45) in Archival Form." *Southeast Asian Studies* (Kyoto (Japan)), vol. 5, no. 2, Center for Southeast Asian Studies, Kyoto University, 2016, pp. 187-218, doi: 10.20495/seas.5.2_187.

"Map of Indochina Showing Proposed Burma-Siam-China Railway." *Scottish Geographical Magazine*, edited by Hugh A. Webster and Arthur S. White, 1886.

Marr, David G. *Vietnam 1945: The Quest for Power.* Berkeley: University of California Press, 1995.

Meurisse, Louis. *Nguyen Aïn Nuä'C (Ho-Chi-Minh), délégué indochinois, Congrès communiste de Marseille.* Bibliothèque Nationale de France Gallica, 1921. https://commons.wikimedia.org/wiki/File:Nguyen_A%C3%AFn_Nu%C3%A4%27C_(Ho-Chi-Minh),_d%C3%A9l%C3%A9gu%C3%A9_indochinois,_Congr%C3%A8s_communiste_de_Marseille,_1921,_Meurisse,_BNF_Gallica.jpg.

Ngô, Vĩnh Long. *Before the Revolution: The Vietnamese Peasants Under the French.* Cambridge, Mass: MIT Press, 1973.

Nguyen, The Anh. "Japanese Food Policies and the 1945 Great Famine in Indochina." In *Food Supplies and the Japanese Occupation in South-East Asia*, edited by Paul H. Kratsoka, 9-31. Palgrave Macmillan UK, 2016.

Nørlund, Irene. "Rice and the Colonial Lobby: The Economic Crisis in French Indo-China in the 1920s and 1930s." In *Weathering the Storm: The Economies of Southeast Asia in the 1930s Depression*, edited by Peter Boomgaard and Ian Brown, Institute of Southeast Asian Studies, Singapore 2000,198-228.

Patti, Archimedes. *Why Viet Nam? Prelude to America's Albatross*. Berkeley: University of California Press, 1980.

Phuong, Hoang. "Nạn Đói Lịch Sử Năm Ất Dậu" [Historical Famine in the Year of the Rooster]. *VnExpress*, 1 Dec. 2015, www.vnexpress.net/nan-doi-lich-su-nam-at-dau-3130107.html.

Richburg, Keith B. "Near Famine in '88, Vietnam Now Exports Rice." *The Washington Post* (1974-Current file); Apr 19, 1990; ProQuest Historical Newspapers: The Washington Post, pg. A37.

Sen, Amartya. *Poverty and Famines: An Essay on Entitlement and Deprivation*. India, Oxford University Press, 1999.

Spector, Ronald H. *Advice and Support: The Early Years, 1941 to 1960*. Washington DC: Center of Military History, 1985.

Tuan, Cam Anh. "The Hải Phòng-Yunnan Railway: An Important Knot in French Indochina-Japanese Relations during the Second World War." In *Vietnam-Indochina-Japan Relations during the Second World War: Documents and Interpretations*, edited by Masaya Shiraishi, Nguyễn Văn Khánh, and Bruce M. Lockhart, 251-257. Waseda University Institute of Asia-Pacific Studies, 2017.

Unknown. *Viet Minh during August Revolution*. 1945. https://commons.wikimedia.org/wiki/File:Viet_Minh_during_August_Revolution.jpg.

Unknown. *Cochinchina uprising (Nam Kỳ Khởi Nghĩa) against the French in Saigon, 1940*. 1940. https://www.flickr.com/photos/13476480@N07/44919600194.

U.S. Army. *Ho Chi Minh (third from left standing) and the OSS in 1945*, 1945. https://commons.wikimedia.org/wiki/File:Ho_Chi_Minh_(third_from_left_standing)_and_the_OSS_in_1945.jpg.

Vallishayee, Rijuta. *A Rough Outline of the Divisions Between Tonkin, Annam, and Cochinchina*. 2021.

—. *Nghe Tinh*. 2021.

—. *The Two Primary Deltas of Vietnam*. 2021.

Van Nguyen-Marshall. "The Moral Economy of Colonialism: Subsistence and Famine Relief in French Indo-China, 1906-1917." *The International History Review*, vol. 27, no. 2, 2005, pp. 237-258. JSTOR, www.jstor.org/stable/40109535. Accessed 13 June 2021.

"Vietnam People's Army Introduction." Ministry of National Defence, Socialist Republic of Vietnam. http://mod.gov.vn/wps/portal/!ut/p/b1/04_Sj9CP ykssy0xPLMnMz0vMAfGjzOLdHP2CLJwMHQ

38zT3dDDy9XL2Nff0NDA0cjYEKIoEKDHAAR wNC-sP1o8BKnN0dPUzMfQwMLHzcTQ08HT 1CgywDjY1BSiAK8Fjh55Gfm6pfkBthkGXiqAgA-8J365g!!/dl4/d5/L2dBISEvZ0FBIS9nQSEh/.

Vo, An Ninh *Famine in Vietnam, 1945.* Museum of Vietnamese History, Hanoi, 1945.

http://www.thanhniennews.com/arts-culture/horrific-photos-recall-vietnamese-famine-of-1945-37591.html.

www.ingramcontent.com/pod-product-compliance
Lightning Source LLC
Chambersburg PA
CBHW060203050426
42446CB00013B/2976